HOW TO KEEP FROM BEING
Robbed, Raped & Ripped Off

HOW TO KEEP FROM BEING

Robbed,

Raped & and

Ripped Off;

A Personal Crime Prevention Manual for You and Your Loved Ones.

By Richard A. Fike
illustrations by Fred Fuldauer
photographs by Randy L. Purdy

ACROPOLIS BOOKS LTD.

WASHINGTON, D.C.

[c1983]

362.88

ACROPOLIS BOOKS, LTD.
Colortone Building, 2400 17th St., N.W.
Washington, D.C. 20009

Printed in the United States of America by
COLORTONE PRESS
Creative Graphics, Inc.
Washington, D.C. 20009

Attention: Schools and Corporations
ACROPOLIS books are available at quantity discounts with bulk purchase for educational, business, or sales promotional use. For information, please write to: SPECIAL SALES DEPARTMENT, ACROPOLIS BOOKS LTD., 2400 17th ST., N.W., WASHINGTON, D.C. 20009.

**Are there Acropolis Books you want
but cannot find in your local stores?**
You can get any Acropolis book title in print. Simply send title and retail price, plus 50 cents per copy to cover mailing and handling costs for each book desired. District of Columbia residents add applicable sales tax. Enclose check or money order only, no cash please, to: ACROPOLIS BOOKS LTD., 2400 17th ST., N.W., WASHINGTON, D.C. 20009.

Library of Congress Cataloging in Publication Data

Fike, Richard A., 1955-
  How to keep from being robbed, raped & ripped off.

  Bibliography: p.
  Includes index.
    1. Crime prevention—United States.   2. Victims of crime—Services for—United States.   3. Self-defense.
I. Title.
HV7431.F48   1983   362.8'8   83-15586
ISBN 0-87491-726-3
ISBN 0-87491-729-8 (pbk.)

Contents

What to do if your child is assaulted...
Kidnapping, custodial abduction, pushouts/
throwaways and runaways... How to locate and
identify your child... If your child is missing...
Tips for parents... Muggers, purse snatchers and
pickpockets... Senior citizens... Submission vs.
resistance

Dedication

To my wife, Linda, whose patience, encouragement
and understanding guided me to the completion of this project.

Acknowledgments

This project could not have been successfully completed without the support and assistance of my friends, associates, and family. Although it is impossible to mention everyone who contributed to this book, I want to acknowledge those who were directly responsible for its completion.

First and foremost, I want to thank my cousin Ted Fike for his interest and sincere belief in the need for a book of this nature, and for introducing me to my publisher Alphons J. Hackl. Special thanks are also extended to my family, who were there when I needed honest criticism as well as support. Many thanks to Thomas P. Daquila, a close friend and associate, for his assistance in reviewing and editing the initial manuscript prior to its submission. I want to express my wholehearted gratitude and appreciation to the following individuals who, each in their own way, increased the professionalism of this book: Richard A. Cermak, Vice President of Security for Fisher Foods, Inc., Bedford Heights, Ohio; Jeff Winton, Administrative Assistant for the Ashtabula County Joint Vocational School, Ashtabula, Ohio; Daniel F. Ponstingle, Coordinator of the Police In-Service Training Program, Lakeland Community College, Mentor, Ohio; Lee G. Feathers, Executive Vice President for Associate Security, Inc., Mentor, Ohio; Charles F. Martin, Director of the Forensic Investigation Service, Painesville, Ohio; Carl Heikkinen, OWE instructor for the Ashtabula County Joint Vocational School, Ashtabula, Ohio; Noah Thomas and Fred Fuldauer of the Crime Prevention Bureau, Mentor Police Department, Mentor, Ohio; Randy L. Purdy, Wooster, Ohio police officer and freelance photographer; Stewart Simonds and Sam King of Photography

Unlimited, Inc., Wooster, Ohio; Leon Hodkey, Eastlake Police Department, Eastlake, Ohio; Charles A. Sutherland, publisher of SEARCH, Englewood Cliffs, New Jersey; and Kristin Cole Brown, Information Director of Child Find, Inc., New Paltz, New York. Thanks also to my private students of the Madison Combined Martial Arts Association: Mary Anne Johnson, Jeffrey L. Powers, Roger D. Fike and his son Matthew Fike, Alan D. Thorne, Edward L. Mementowski, Carmine Petecca, Mike and Wendy Gerlica, Karen Nowosadski, Mike Izzarelli, and Kirk Kidner. Also, I wish to thank the entire staff of Acropolis Books: Alphons J. Hackl, Muriel Hackl, Jody L. Peskin, Kathleen Hughes, Sandy Trupp, Laurie Dustman Tag, Jennifer Prost, John Hackl, Eileen Tansill, Sharon Smith, Robert Hickey, Christopher Jones, Laurie Richardson, Irma Gallagher, Katherine Smith and editor, Valerie Avedon. Last but not least, I want to thank the good Lord above for his strength and guidance in writing this book.

CHAPTER ONE

Crime in the United States: Don't Become a Statistic

Much crime can be prevented.

The amount of crime we are experiencing in the United States today is frightening. It is especially disheartening to hear how much of it could have been prevented if only the necessary precautions had been taken. We all run the risk of becoming a victim at least once during our lifetime; for many of us, the odds are even greater.

Someone is murdered in the United States every 23 minutes, robbed every 55 seconds, and seriously assaulted every 49 seconds. It seems that at least one newspaper story appears each day about a rape, assault, kidnapping, or similar crime in each of our neighborhoods. Perhaps you even know the victim involved. When we hear about a violent crime, our first reaction is one of disgust. Then we silently thank the good Lord that it did not involve a member of our own family. But what if it had? What if your son or daughter had been attacked, injured, or even killed? Feelings of anger, rage, and helplessness quickly follow. Now you have to become involved. How guilty would you feel if it were too late to do something to save your child? Unfortunately, this "after the fact" attitude, rather than the attitude of prevention, seems to prevail. In many cases people blame society, or express outrage that the police failed to prevent certain crimes. We cannot expect law enforcement agencies in our communities to stop all crime in its tracks. It's always easier to look back and point out what went wrong than to look into the future to know who will be the next victim, or what the risks are in each of our lives. We can, however, establish effective countermeasures against crime. When perfected, these countermeasures can increase our safety and that of our loved ones.

Crime affects literally every segment of society. It can strike out at anyone at any time. We cannot choose when we would like to be attacked. There is no taking a number, and there is never a "better" time to be assaulted. Study the following chart. Its statistics can give you an idea of the incidence of murder, robbery, and aggravated assaults in the area where you live.

The Key to Survival is Awareness

This book will help you avoid becoming one of those statistics. The key to survival is to establish the necessary safeguards and take the preventative measures to eliminate or at least limit the opportunity for crime. You can become difficult to attack, or simply not worth the attacker's trouble. As selfish as it may sound, you want the criminal to look elsewhere for a victim. Former criminals, as well as those on the streets today, will tell you that their targets all tend to exhibit certain weak characteristics. It's common sense to choose a target that you feel confident you can defeat. In many cases, victims often attract or invite assault because of the way they walk, talk, and dress. Walking with your head down, unsure or uncoordinated in your movements, signifies a possible lack of confidence. This could happen when walking through a new shopping plaza, or an unfamiliar city block—your body language can alert potential muggers to approaching prey. The reverse can be true of a person who walks with a smooth, even stride. Coordination increases with relaxation. Relaxation increases with confidence. Add the fact that this person's head is erect, and that he is aware of all activity in his vicinity, and you now have a person who would not be considered an easy mark. The assailant alert to these positive body cues, would probably decide to look elsewhere for a more susceptible target. Developing and maintaining a positive and confident attitude is really not difficult. When you understand and analyze the activities that surround you, you'll find that your confidence grows and radiates. This positive attitude is a plus for you, and a minus for the criminal

Crime does not always choose its victims by their affluence. It often strikes out at the first person in its path—some poor soul in the wrong place at the right time. This is why we must learn to expect the unexpected if we want to be prepared to face any possible situation.

Although most of the criminals who infect our society choose a life of crime freely, in many cases society is to blame. What deters the criminal from his wrong doings? In some cases it can be the establishment, strictly enforcing the law. In other cases social reform affects each member of that society. Threat of strict punishment can prevent crime in some cases, and a return to crime in others. Unfortunately, crime can never be completely eliminated. We must accept this fact and prepare to meet it whenever it should come to call.

This book cannot answer all your questions. I don't think any one book could. It does provide recommendations and procedures for you to use in developing effective preventative measures or strengthening already established procedures.

It's Up To You To Get Involved

By choosing to read this book you have already shown a concern for crime prevention. The next step is to apply what you have learned. Nobody is going to do it for you. Too often a book is read and then stuck back on the shelf, destined for a life of dust and cobwebs, as though the reader had memorized its contents.

Three Priorities

The guidelines established in this book follow a simple, logical set of priorities:

Priority I. Avoid all hostile situations. Through careful study of our daily environments we can learn what threats exist and begin to establish effective preventative measures to deter them. When we increase our awareness of our surroundings and make a conscious effort to sharpen our reactions, we learn to remain calm—not to panic in stress situations and thereby lose the chance to react sensibly and properly. Education and training are crucial to proper prevention.

Priority II. When necessary, and only as a last resort, we must be able to apply defensive tactics if attacked. Once we're faced with a threatening situation, we must be able to assume a defensive attitude (or to switch to an offensive attitude if need be) to overwhelm an aggressor and escape.

Priority III. After reading this book thoroughly, try to add some effective procedures to assist you and your family. Continue to look for weaknesses in your lifestyle, and develop counter-measures to strengthen your position. Above all, don't limit yourself to a few half-attempted ideas that may only get you into more trouble. Remember that the education process continues throughout our lifetimes. Those who seek a better way to accomplish a task will eventually find it. For your sake and for your family's sake, never stop seeking the answers.

I think you will find that the techniques described here will enable you to fight back intelligently, to win the sometimes unavoidable battle before it begins, and, in many cases, to do so "without firing a shot." We'll begin with ways to avoid crime in your home, your work place, your school, and your leisure environment. Then, and only then will we study defense techniques because I strongly believe they should only be used when all else fails.

As the old Chinese proverb says, "Learn the ways to preserve rather than destroy. Avoid rather than check, check rather than hurt, hurt rather than maim, maim rather than kill . . . for all life is precious nor can any be replaced." To fight for what you believe in is honorable, but to fight when there is no hope of winning, or when there is a more sensible action to take is foolish.

CRIME STATISTICS CHART

What Do Crime Statistics Say About Your Area?

Murders
(per 100,000 population)

Miami	61
St. Louis	58
Newark	49
Atlanta	43
Detroit	42
Cleveland	41
New Orleans	39
Oakland	35
Washington, D.C.	35
Birmingham	34
Dallas	33
Los Angeles	30
Fort Worth	29
Chicago	29
Baltimore	29
New York	26
Kansas City, M.	26
San Antonio	24
Philadelphia	21
Memphis	21
Long Beach	20
Denver	20
San Francisco	19
Louisville	18
Boston	18
Nashville	17
Jacksonville	16
Charlotte	16
Oklahoma City	18
Columbus	16
Toledo	15
Tulsa	14
Albuquerque	14
Phoenix	12
Seattle	12
Pittsburgh	12
Austin	11
Milwaukee	11
Honolulu	11
Cincinnati	11
San Jose	11
San Diego	11
Buffalo	10
Portland, Oreg.	10
Indianapolis	9
Omaha	9
Tucson	8
El Paso	8
Minneapolis	8

Robberies
(per 100,000 population)

Newark	2,362
Miami	1,786
Boston	1,643
Washington, D.C.	1,631
New York	1,520
Cleveland	1,363
Baltimore	1,362
Detroit	1,230
St. Louis	1,184
Oakland	1,131
San Francisco	1,088
Atlanta	1,060
Pittsburgh	1,011
Los Angeles	949
New Orleans	888
Portland, Oreg.	839
Long Beach	810
Kansas City, Mo.	722
Philadelphia	641
Memphis	633
Minneapolis	619
Forth Worth	600
Dallas	598
Columbus	594
Buffalo	592
Louisville	580
Chicago	536
Birmingham	528
Toledo	501
Denver	489
Seattle	475
Cincinnati	456
Jacksonville	433
San Diego	380
Oklahoma City	370
Honolulu	362
Nashville	350
Phoenix	341
Albuquerque	334
San Jose	325
Indianapolis	313
Omaha	288
Milwaukee	284
Tucson	264
Tulsa	263
Charlotte	246
San Antonio	234
El Paso	205
Austin	194

Aggravated Assaults
(per 100,000 population)

Miami	1,275
Atlanta	1,234
Newark	1,149
St. Louis	954
Kansas City, Mo.	878
Portland, Oreg.	802
Baltimore	792
Oakland	782
Boston	745
Los Angeles	712
Charlotte	682
Dallas	656
Cleveland	654
New York	619
El Paso	551
San Francisco	564
Oklahoma City	555
Detroit	542
Fort Worth	542
Washington, D.C.	538
Tucson	529
Jacksonville	517
Seattle	511
Birmingham	501
Albuquerque	488
Cincinnati	468
New Orleans	449
Buffalo	435
Denver	430
Tulsa	398
Phoenix	395
Long Beach	351
Pittsburgh	338
Philadelphia	326
Minneapolis	321
Memphis	320
San Diego	299
San Antonio	287
Indianapolis	268
Louisville	264
Columbus	251
Chicago	245
San Jose	239
Nashville	231
Milwaukee	198
Toledo	185
Austin	166
Omaha	151
Honolulu	93

Source: U.S. Department of Justice, Uniform Crime Report, Crime in the USA 1981/82.

Crime in the United States: Don't Become a Statistic

CHAPTER TWO

Recognizing Threats in Your Home Environment

Evelyn left her garden apartment to run out for some charcoal to barbecue some steaks that night.

"I don't need to lock the sliding glass door out back," she thought to herself, "I'll only be gone a few minutes."

An hour later, Evelyn returned to a ransacked apartment—gone were her camera, stereo, portable TV, the steaks, and her hibachi! Luckily, the steaks were the only things not marked with her social security number, so if any of the stolen items are recovered, she should get them back. But Evelyn will never again leave the back door open for "just a minute."

Throughout most of our daily routine, we find ourselves or members of our family, in, or between, one of four basic environments: *home, work, school* or *recreational*. By carefully studying these environments on an individual basis, we can identify the special threats and vulnerabilities that are unique to each of the four and establish effective preventative procedures against them. Once prevention has been instituted, we can move in a positive direction to create a far more controlled environment than previously thought. We are prepared to handle the situations that arise by being knowledgeable of the crises that are likely to affect us in each environment.

It's next to impossible to know where crime will strike. Naturally, if we knew, we could avoid it. Because, however, we cannot always avoid crime, we must be prepared to deter or stop it. To do so requires sound prevention; it may also call for the application of defensive tactics.

We are all concerned about securing our homes or apartments from criminals. After all, we like to think of our homes as our castles, affording us safety and protection from the elements. Most of us are aware of the need to protect our homes, but seldom do we actually take necessary precautionary measures. Many feel that it's too costly; others simply don't take the time or make the effort to establish minimal preventative measures. It's one thing to come home and discover that someone has stolen your television set and stereo, make out a police report, and call the insurance company. It's another thing altogether to be caught at home when the criminal breaks through your back door. What if someone tries to break into your house while your children and the babysitter are there? Who is this intruder? What should you do to deter him?

There are two main types of burglars. One is the professional thief who spends much time studying, or "casing," your residence. He looks for your patterns of activity, and selects the prime time to enter. In most cases, the victims provided the burglar with easy access through unlocked doors or windows, or even by leaving a key under the mat. The professional's moves are usually undetected and he is careful not to leave any clues behind. He will generally escape unnoticed, never to be caught. The amateur is, in most cases, the juvenile who needs quick money. He moves directly into the residence, often by breaking windows or doors. This amateur thief is usually very nervous and clumsy as he searches for money or things that can be sold quickly (stereo, camera, television set).

Neither criminal wants to be detected, but in most cases the amateur is probably the most dangerous. When he is surprised by a resident he may panic, and run, shoot, or stab the occupant out of fear. The professional is likely to flee before confronting an occupant.

Time is of the essence to a criminal. The less time involved in an illegal act, the better. If you make it tougher for a housebreaker to enter by increasing the time it takes him to gain access he may well choose another, more vulnerable, target.

Thirty percent of homes and residences in the United States

were scenes of crime in 1981. The odds are pretty good that you or a friend or relative could become a target. More than 20 percent of American households were affected by larceny in 1981, and approximately 7 percent were broken into. However, 1982 figures indicate a 10 percent decrease in burglaries and a 1 percent decrease in larcenies, indicating that crime prevention is beginning to have a positive affect against crime.

Internal and External Protection

Read the following checklist to determine how vulnerable your home or apartment is to crime. Once you identify the weaknesses, you can begin to correct or reinforce them to meet minimum security requirements. If you're looking for a home to rent or buy, drive through the area and talk with neighbors and business people. Do this at night, and on weekends, to see what type of activity exists.

If you live in an apartment, contact the manager or landlord to assist in the survey. You might even remind him that by increasing safeguards he can probably save on his insurance premiums!

Residential Survey Questions

1. How much security currently exists?
2. How effective is existing security?
3. What threats could affect you?
4. What crime has already occurred?
5. How much/what type of crime exists in this neighborhood?
6. How long does it take for local police, fire, and rescue services to arrive?
7. Do the local police monitor residential alarms? What is their response time?
8. Does a commercial company monitor residential alarms? What is its response time?
9. How much can you afford to spend on increasing home security?

External Home Security Checklist

1. What is your location in relation to neighbors or businesses? Establish complete boundaries and perimeters of residences. Use photos, illustrations, maps.

2. Is your house or apartment number visible from the street, 24 hours a day, for emergency service? If not, consider placing it in plain view.
3. What type of landscaping surrounds your residence?
   - Does it block the view of the driveway or garage?
   - Do bushes, hedges, or fences provide cover for a criminal near windows, doors, or sidewalks?
   - Do trees, existing buildings, fences, or flower trellises provide access onto a roof, ledge, or balcony?
4. What barriers border your residence?
   - Are there fences? Do they have gates that secure and operate effectively?
   - Are there walls from other buildings?
   - Are there natural barriers such as hedges?
   - Are there vehicles (e.g., trucks) parked nearby that afford entry over perimeter barriers?
5. What type of lighting exists?
   - Are there street lights? Do they work?
   - Do existing lights provide complete and adequate coverage to all entrances, exits, parking lots, driveways, etc.?
   - Have you considered lights that turn on automatically at dusk, and off at dawn?
   - Is there an alternate light source or back-up lighting system?
6. Are there any additional buildings or sheds, and are they secured properly?
7. Where are the external fuse or power boxes?
8. Are fuse/power boxes locked securely?
9. Is the telephone cable accessible from the ground?
10. Does the garage door open, close, and lock properly?
11. Are all unused doors and windows permanently locked?
12. Are all ladders and lawn furniture secured inside?
13. Is there a guard dog?
    - Is the guard dog secured?
    - Is the guard dog protected from the weather?
    - Are there "Beware of Dog" signs posted?
14. Are the vehicles parked outside your residence locked, and the windows rolled up tight?

15. Are access keys located outside hidden in obvious locations?
16. If female, and living alone, is your full name (preceded by Ms., Miss, or Mrs.) listed on your mail box? Use your first and middle initials only, with your last name, in order not to alert would-be criminals that you are alone.
17. Are keys for all external locks marked and maintained in a safe and accessible location inside the residence?

Internal Home Security Checklist

1. Does each room, including hallways and stairs, have an adequate lighting system? Are timers used when on vacation? Are they safe?
2. Is there an auxiliary lighting back-up system?
3. Are flashlights and charged batteries stored in each room?
4. Does each room have window blinds or shades?
5. Is there a first-aid kit, with a manual, in the house?
6. Are internal doors equipped with locking devices?
7. Can these doors be opened from outside the room in the event a child is locked in?
8. Are smoke alarms installed and working?
9. Is there a fire exit plan? Are all residents aware of it?
10. If residing in an apartment complex, do main outer doors lock, requiring resident keys to open them?
11. Are there fire extinguishers where needed?
12. Where is the internal fuse/power box located?
    - Is the fuse/power box reachable?
    - Are extra fuses available?
13. Do all telephones have emergency phone numbers (police, fire and rescue, poison control center) posted on or near them?
14. Are weapons stored inside the home?
    - Are all family members aware of weapons and their location?
    - Are weapons stored in a safe location to prevent accidental discovery?
15. Is there a complete inventory list of all property, with extra copies stored in a safe deposit box and with the insurance company?
16. Is there a security room designated?

17. Does the security room contain all the necessary emergency supplies?
18. Is there a security safe or fire resistant steel box for important papers, documents, and valuables?
    • Who knows where the safe is?
    • Who knows the safe combination?

Apartment/College Campus Tips

1. Who else has keys that will fit your residence/room?
2. Will management/college re-key your doors?
3. Will management/college let you pay for this service? (It is still worth it, even if you have to pay for it yourself.)
4. How secure are existing door and window locks?
5. Are all stairways, hallways, and surrounding property well lighted?
6. Where is the laundry room? Is it well lighted and secured?
7. Does your apartment or campus building have an emergency fire alarm? Does it work? Where is the fire exit?

Locking Devices

Most residences can be entered with little or no force. As mentioned earlier, many people go to great lengths to obtain expensive locking systems, only to leave their doors and windows unlocked. No home can be completely burglar-proofed, but you can reduce the chances of a break-in.

Some homes are secured with only a spring-latch door lock that can be pried open within seconds. Check your locks by opening the door and locking the lock device (usually by pushing in a button). Next, try to push in the bolt that locks into the door frame when it's closed. If the bolt slides back into the door, you have a spring-latch lock. If at all possible, replace this lock with a deadbolt lock, or even better, add a deadbolt in addition to the existing lock. If your door is fitted improperly to the door frame (leaving a narrow gap) there is the possibility of a criminal popping, jimmying, or prying the locking bolt from the doorstrike. If possible, replace door frames with new metal frames, and old doors with solid hardwood or metal, especially if you are building your home.

If the lock bolt and the lock strike are strong, the criminal sometimes attempts to pry the door off its hinges. Check to insure that hinge screws are not stripped and that they are tightly and properly secured. In most cases, it's probably very easy to lift the hinge pin from the hinge and enter through this side of the door. So be sure to keep all hinges facing inward, with the door swinging in. You can improve door security if you remove the center screw from each side of the existing hinge, drill each hole to a depth of ½ inch, and place a headless screw or pin on one side (figure 2-1). When the door is closed, the end of the screw or pin will seat itself into the empty screw hole. If the hinge pins are removed, the door will still be bolted to the frame.

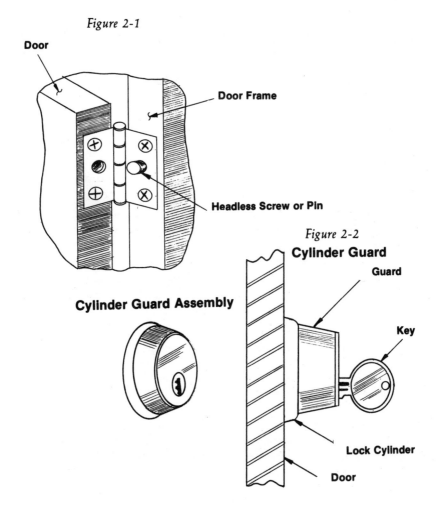

Figure 2-1

Door

Door Frame

Headless Screw or Pin

Figure 2-2

Cylinder Guard

Cylinder Guard Assembly

Guard

Key

Lock Cylinder

Door

Deadbolts offer just about the highest degree of security you can expect, short of Fort Knox. Deadbolt locks can only be opened by a key or a key-turn knob. There are different qualities of deadbolts on the market today, so it's important to choose one made of case-hardened steel, which resists cutting.

You can reinforce the door-frame strike to provide maximum strength. The strike plate should be attached to the door frame with screws at least three inches long. Make sure that the bolt, when locked, seats at least five-eighths of an inch in the doorjamb. Also be sure that the cylinder of the lock has a steel guard (a ring around the key section) that's tapered around the key slot to keep it from being wrenched off (Figure 2-2). Secure the lock cylinder with five or six pin tumblers to provide more resistance against picking, although very few residences are entered by the lock-picking method. Lock-picking requires a certain amount of skill, but even the best pickers struggle when picking an old, worn, or damaged lock, so this technique is seldom used.

Two common deadbolt locks are used in most residential facilities. The first is a double-cylinder lock with key entry and exit from both the inside and the outside. The second type (also double cylinder) is operated by a key from the outside and a turn knob from the inside. Consider these points before choosing:

1. If you secure your doors with a double-cylinder lock, remember that you must have a key to open it (when locked) from the inside. This could create a fire hazard in the event of an emergency, so be sure the key is left in place when the house is occupied. Some deadbolt double-cylinder locks have a turn knob/key which, when inserted, acts as a turn knob, but can be removed.

2. During a burglary, a criminal might break through a door, or a window next to the door, to reach in and activate a turnknob type deadbolt. With the double-cylinder lock which has no turnknob, this act would be futile. When you have a double-cylinder deadbolt (minus the turnknob), the burglar would not be able to make a fast exit with large objects because the doors would be secure. If your door or adjacent window provides access to locking devices, replace the glass with break-resistant materials that look like glass and resist cutting. Metal grillwork in also very effective here.

Each door to your home should have a one-way peephole or wide-angle viewer (figure 2-3). Window viewers or small sliding viewers provide you with a fair amount of security when observing and talking to a stranger or delivery man, but even these should be equipped with some form of slide lock or metal grillwork. When possible, install an intercom system, which is the safest form of communication with a visitor. At a minimum, each door should have a slide chain and latch firmly secured to the door and door frame. This slide chain allows you to open the door enough to sign for mail or talk with visitors. Evaluate the security and effectiveness of all door hardware and apply the necessary safeguards.

Double Doors

When securing double doors, be sure that the stationary door is properly equipped with bolts at top and bottom (Figure 2-4). The operational or opening door should have a deadbolt lock feature as previously discussed.

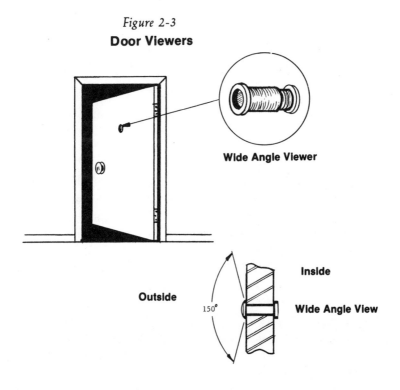

Figure 2-3
Door Viewers

Wide Angle Viewer

Outside 150° **Inside**

Wide Angle View

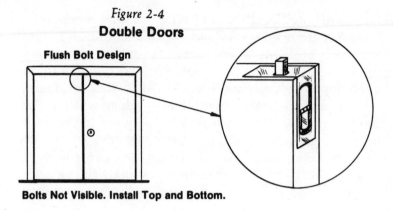

Figure 2-4
Double Doors

Flush Bolt Design

Bolts Not Visible. Install Top and Bottom.

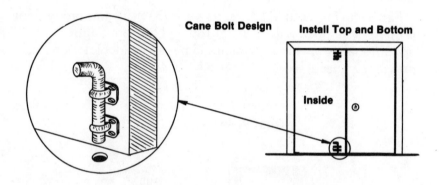

Cane Bolt Design

Install Top and Bottom

Inside

Window Locks

Most windows are easily opened from the outside when not secured with the proper locking devices. When possible, protect all windows with metal grillwork or bars. This is especially important for basement and ground-floor windows. In addition, unbreakable glass or a break-resistant glass substitute can be used to replace or reinforce existing glass. Each individual window should have its own locking mechanism. Use key locks if possible. They mean extra security if the criminal breaks the glass and tries to open a window. But, as with the door frame, if it is old and the wood is rotting, it should be replaced. In addition to existing locks, a simple, effective way to secure double-hung sash windows is to drill a slanted hole through the front (inside) sash, halfway into the rear (outer) sash, and insert a metal pin or nail (Figure 2-5).

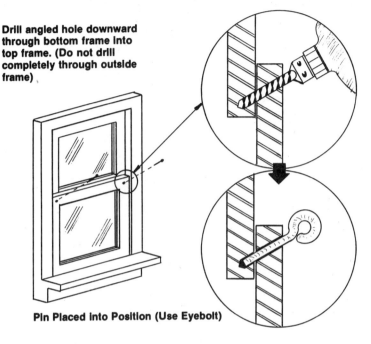

Figure 2-5

Double Hung Sash Windows

Drill angled hole downward through bottom frame into top frame. (Do not drill completely through outside frame)

Pin Placed Into Position (Use Eyebolt)

Another common window lock, especially on older homes, is the lever latch design or casement-window type (Figure 2-6). This type of latch lock is used on metal frame windows and is opened laterally by hand or by crank. It is very easy to push a coat hanger through a worn window frame to push the lever handle free. In most cases, the burglar will simply break the glass, and reach in and open the latch or operate the crank. To prevent this, remove the cranks and keep them nearby for emergencies, or drill a ¼-inch hole through the latch and handle. Next, insert a ¼-inch pin that slides freely in and out of the hole, and cut the ends off flush. Paint the end of the pins so as not to identify their location. If a burglar tries to open the handle he will run into trouble, and since time is of the essence, he may give up. It's very important that all household members be able to remove the pin by pushing it out, or by using a magnet, especially in the event of a fire when immediate evacuation is necessary.

Louvered glass windows are hard to secure because the individual panes are relatively easy to remove, but you can provide the following safeguards to gain added security (see Figure 2-7):

Figure 2-6

Casement Window Latch

¼ inch hole drilled. Pin prevents latch from opening. Pin should be installed flush with latch on either side.

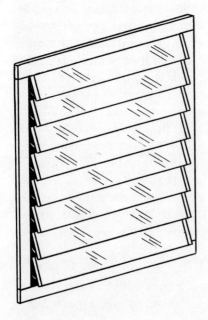

Figure 2-7

Louvered Window

- Glue each window pane and the clips that hold them in the frame. This will slow the removal process of the windows.
- If clips are aluminum (as most are), purchase steel replacement clips. These are more difficult for the burglar to bend, so it's harder for him to remove the glass.
- Apply window grills, grates, or bars. Remember to consider hazards that exist in case of an emergency. Be sure to install quick releases for these guards or plan to use an alternate exit.

Closely examine each window on your property to determine how effective the existing lock is. If it does not have a lock, determine the specific type needed and install it immediately. If necessary, check with a security consultant or your local police for suggestions.

Don't forget—window air conditioning units can be easily pushed in or pulled out of their mounts. Make sure they are securely attached to prevent this.

Sliding Doors/Windows

If your home has sliding doors, you need to be able to secure them effectively. Because most of these doors can be easily pried open, it is important to use a steel rod, commonly called a Charlie Bar, or a length of wood in the door track to keep it from sliding open. Most sliding doors can also be lifted off their tracks. To counter this tactic, place one or more screws into the upper track to provide enough clearance so that the door will slide open, yet cannot be lifted off its tracks. Also, you can drill a diagonal slot down through the top frame into the door and insert a nail or metal pin to keep the door from being opened (Figure 2-8).

Figure 2-8

Sliding Glass (Patio) Door

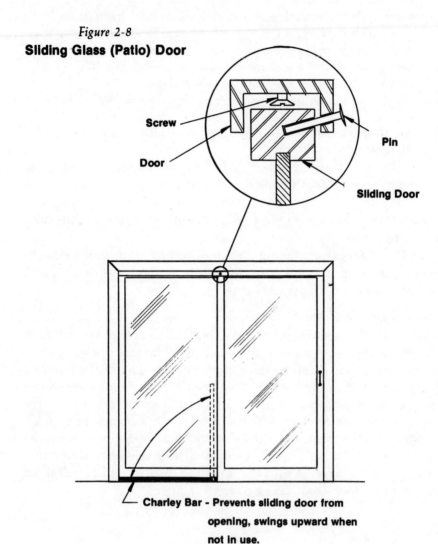

Screw

Door

Pin

Sliding Door

Charley Bar - Prevents sliding door from opening, swings upward when not in use.

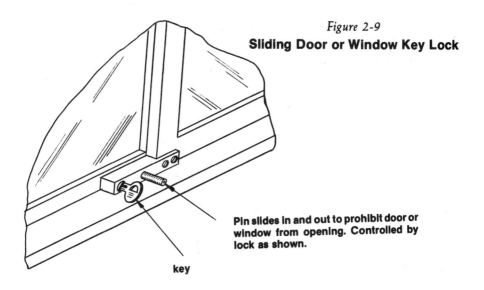

Figure 2-9
Sliding Door or Window Key Lock

Pin slides in and out to prohibit door or window from opening. Controlled by lock as shown.

key

Figure 2-10
Hasp

Screws or bolts exposed when opened.

When closed, screws or bolts secured (hidden).

You can buy and install locks for your sliding doors (Figure 2-9) and windows. Key locks provide excellent protection, but remember to place the key nearby for emergencies.

Padlocks

Outdoor sheds, garage doors, etc., are usually secured with padlocks. If you decide to use one, remember that it, along with a cheap hasp, can be pried or cut off quickly. A padlock should only be used as a deterrent. Always insure that the hasps are strong, secured with bolts, and mounted on a metal plate, and that the bolts are hidden when the lock is applied. Look for a padlock that retains its key when open, to help remind you to lock the padlock before you leave (Figure 2-10).

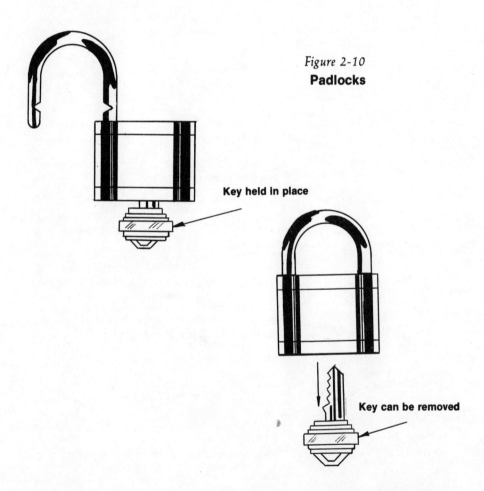

Figure 2-10
Padlocks

Key held in place

Key can be removed

Miscellaneous Openings

Even though you have evaluated and secured your doors and windows, a criminal can still gain entrance through cellar doors, crawl spaces under your floors, and air conditioning and heating system vents and ducts. Secure them appropriately.

One last item: Any time you move into a new home or apartment, chances are that there are other keys floating around which will operate your locks. Consider changing them, or contact a local locksmith to re-key or repin your existing lock system. This can be relatively inexpensive and may prevent the future loss of valuables.

Alarm Systems

When you buy an alarm system, several things should be considered prior to installation. Do you need to secure a residential area or a commercial area? Exactly what is the value of the property and merchandise you wish to protect? Once you have answered these questions, you can more effectively choose a system that's right for you. The alarm systems available on the market today can perform just about any security function. Make sure you understand the degree of protection you need, then look for the system that will afford you this protection. If you own a $250,000 home, it doesn't make much sense to purchase a system for $100 that will provide $100 worth of protection. The opposite is also true. Why place a $3,000 alarm system on your $25,000 home and property when a $1,000 system would be just as effective? It's the old story—don't put a $50 lock on a $2 hasp. The system is only as strong as its weakest link.

With such a wide range of systems to choose from, you should have no trouble finding one that both meets your needs and fits your budget. If you require a special, unique system, there are experts who can design, build, and install it for you. I strongly recommend that you shop around until you find the system best for you. It's quite possible that you don't really need an alarm system, even though it is always a plus for added security. Consider all the facts first. Maybe you simply need to improve your existing security and lighting hardware. Adding a lock here or a light there will greatly increase your overall security, sometimes much more effectively than alarms. After all, an alarm signals only when an intruder is attempting to enter or after he is already inside. If the property is secured in the first place, the criminal may not be able to enter at all.

It is next to impossible to discuss all currently available systems here, but to introduce you to the basics involved, let's briefly look at what constitutes an alarm system and how these systems can be employed.

To begin with, all alarm systems contain *sensors*, whose function is to detect and report disturbances caused by a possible intruder. Most sensors are of electronic, microwave, photo-electric, motion/vibration, audio, or radar design. Most operate by breaking or disturbing an existing electrical current or completing a current. Once an intruder is detected, the sensor signals the adjoining control panel of the unauthorized entry.

The *control panel unit* is the brains of the alarm system. Its job is to receive the sensor signal and trigger a local or central station alarm.

The *alarm* is the device that alerts the operator or monitor to the presence of an intruder. Bells, sirens, horns, etc., are designed to both alert the resident to an unauthorized entry and scare off the intruder. Lights flashing on and off provide a visual alarm system to silently notify both residents and police or security personnel, of the entry attempt.

Many sophisticated systems also automatically turn on lighting systems upon alarm, turn on water sprinkler systems upon activation of heat sensors, turn off air conditioning/freezer systems upon activation of a temperature drop, or turn off heating systems upon a temperature rise.

There are three basic systems of alarm response.

1 **Local Alarm:** This system is designed to alert and warn personnel within a designated area. The alarm can be located on the inside of a building, the outside of a building, or a perimeter wall. This response system would be recommended for a location that is some distance from local police or security guards—a farm barn, for example. It will generally frighten away both unwanted animals and unwanted trespassers.

2. **Central or Remote Stations:** Central or remote stations receive the alarm and dispatch police or security personnel to investigate. Response time is critical, so there are usually officers standing by to respond immediately. These systems are used in banks, retail stores, etc.

3. **Proprietary.** This system is designed to receive the alarm on the secured site and is handled within the protected location by an established security force. It is used by large warehouses and apartment complexes to provide security to property and residents.

Alarm systems are either powered by battery (wireless) or by a power source that utilizes wiring (plug-in/generator type), with battery back-up if the main power source is cut. As a rule, your system should include a fire sensing device, and a way to gauge how the system is operating (i.e., poor, weak, dead).

Most alarms are placed at either the perimeter of the area to be protected or within the area itself. Perimeter alarms are used on gates, fences, doors, windows, and other related entrances. They include, but are not limited to, electromechanical (circuit design), contact magnetic detectors, glass systems, and electrical switches that are recessed into doors, gates, and windows, and are activated when released.

Interior alarms are set up to detect sound and motion within an established area. They can be motion detection devices (ultrasonic, sonic, and microwave), vibration and seismic (effected by local disturbance), photoelectric cells (usually infrared type) that establish a beam of non-visible light between two designated points, and audio or acoustic alarm systems that can pick up the sound of a pin dropping.

Costs

Local alarm systems can be purchased from between $10 and $2,000. You could probably build one yourself if you are electrically inclined; but if you do, be sure that it functions properly if you want to save a lot of headaches and frustration later.

Central or remote systems can be installed for from $100 to $3,000, depending on your needs. Once installed, there is usually a monthly monitoring fee that can range from $25 to $75. It's best to have experts determine your exact needs, but whichever system you purchase, make sure that it is Underwriters' Laboratories–approved! If you do decide to install an alarm system, check with your insurance company for discount rates.

Proprietary system expenses vary widely, depending on the cost of employing an established local guard force.

Safes or Fire-Resistant Steel Boxes

Safes

Every home and commercial business should have a security safe to protect such highly valuable items as jewels, stocks and bonds, and large sums of cash from burglars. There are many different safes on the market today designed to resist forceful entrance. A well-designed safe should have:

- heavy gauge steel walls, top, bottom, and door;
- fire resistant/retardant material lining its walls; and
- a three position, dial type, combination locking device.

When contemplating the purchase of a safe, read all accompanying paperwork thoroughly to determine exactly to what specifications the safe is designed and how secure it is against fire and theft.

The steel used in most safes is designed to resist a certain amount of forceful beating or burning by torches. If a safe or cabinet is not designed to withstand a predetermined amount of heat, you can expect most flammable items inside to burn up if torched, so it's a good idea to find one that is heat-resistant. Many descriptions of containers say they are burglar- and fire-proof. Do not take the description literally. Although safes are resistant to a certain amount of applied force and heat, all safes can be entered, given enough time, and they can also be burned through or melted with extreme heat. Consider your specific needs, and be sure it's Underwriters' Laboratories–approved.

The purpose of safes is to protect valuables from theft and fire, but they are often merely deterrents for the amateur, and a time-consumer for the professional. If he wants to get in, he will, but there are certain measures you can take to improve the security of your safe.

- Chain it to a permanent fixture with a high-security chain and lock.
- Hide home safes in a nonvisible locale and tell no one but family members of their existence. Commercial safes should be placed in open, visible, well lighted areas that can be observed through windows. This prevents burglars

from attempting entry unobserved and allows the safe to be visually checked by passing police or security.

- Maintain strict confidentiality of the combination. The combinations of most purchased safes can be changed by the owner, with no need for a locksmith.
- If it is a commercial safe, use an appropriate alarm system that will alert police or security to a burglary attempt. There are many systems available that are activated by pressure, sound, or heat. Consult an expert on your specific needs.

Security Room

When possible, every home should have a specific room that can provide a high degree of protection to the whole family. "Security rooms" are usually designed to hide residents from intruders, but are never to be used as a refuge against fire. A good example of a home that should have a security room is one that is any great distance from the police. If you are building a home, be sure to include a room of this nature. In an older home, closet space can be converted for this purpose. As a last resort, a central room which is equipped with interior locks and a telephone can serve as a security room. All security rooms should include the following characteristics/supplies:

- The door should be solid hardwood, preferably steel, and should be kept secured at all times to prevent children from locking themselves in.
- The door and door frame should be reinforced.
- An interior lock should be added.
- The outside of the door should not identify the room, if at all possible.
- There should be a light switch to control external lights.
- The room should have adequate internal lighting.
- The telephone's ringer should be tuned down, or removed and replaced with a light. Emergency numbers should be posted.
- Food, water, blankets, first aid and medical supplies, any special medication unique to family members, flashlight and portable radio/TV with batteries, electric socket to provide electricity, and sanitary supplies should be on hand. These could include a weapon if desired.
- The room should have adequate ventilation.
- An escape door should be provided if possible.

Remember that you may have to remain in the room for up to one or two days, so maintain adequate supplies. Check the room and supplies for effectiveness periodically and schedule test runs for family members. It is important never to discuss the existence of a security room with anyone except immediate family members.

Family Security Procedures

Education begins in the home. You and your family should seriously study each other's lifestyles, be it work or school and point out potential dangers. Your son or daughter may have unique knowledge of a certain threat of which you are unaware. Everyone should listen and participate. By getting everyone involved, you can get a fairly good idea of the areas of concern facing your family.

Hold meetings to discuss any new ideas, thereby emphasizing the importance of prevention. Strive to develop an attitude of prevention. Once good security practices are developed into habits, your children can carry them over into their own families.

As soon as they are old enough to understand, children should be taught:

- Never to talk with strangers;
- Never accept gifts from strangers;
- Never get into a stranger's car;
- Report strangers or suspicious activity to their parents, babysitter, and police immediately;
- Always play in pairs;
- Never open the door without a parent's permission;
- Never hitchhike;
- Always inform their parents where they will be, for how long, and with whom.

The Telephone

The easiest way to gain information not otherwise available is by using the telephone. Anyone who combines a little tact, courtesy, and charm with bits and pieces of previously gathered facts (to make the caller sound legitimate) can usually persuade an individual to provide the requested information. This includes telephone operators. For this reason, it is of the utmost importance to train all family members, secretaries, maids, baby-sitters, etc., on how and what to say over the phone.

To start with, it might not be a bad idea to request an unlisted telephone number. You can provide your number to your friends and relatives while keeping the random caller off the line. If a call is important, there are emergency methods of locating you through the operator. Provide all associated employments, schools, hospitals, etc., with your number when possible. Request a one-party line.

Recommendations

- Never provide your name or phone number to a person calling whom you think has the wrong number. Ask him what number he wants, and politely say, "Sorry, this is not that number." If the caller persists, hang up immediately.
- Never answer questions asked by strangers over the phone, especially those who request personal information, such as what bank you deal with, how much money you have in your savings, or your account numbers. Many gimmicks are used to get you to give out important financial information over the phone.
- Beware of a caller identifying himself as an employee of your bank, stating that they have had a computer breakdown and need some pertinent information on your checking/savings accounts. In a case like this, always request the caller's name and number and tell him you will return his call. Do not use the number that the caller has provided, but look up the number of your bank in your phone directory and use that one if they are indeed different. Ask to speak to the bank manager or the head teller and explain your situation. If the call was legitimate, they will know of it. If not, notify the police immediately.
- Never disclose over the phone that you are alone.
- Never discuss time schedules or vacation schedules.
- If you are a female living alone, do not list your full name in the phone directory. Use just your first and middle initial with your last name. Many crank callers pick on women who live alone.
- Never keep your phone off the hook. You never know who is attempting to call you in case of an emergency.
- Never become trapped into providing information to female callers. Females are used in many cases to elicit information because of their soft, persuasive voices.
- Do not be tricked into providing information to someone

saying, "Congratulations, you have just won a new car, television set, or microwave oven! Please confirm for us your phone number, address, etc." Always ask them to identify themselves and who they represent, and make sure you have entered the contest that you have just won. Most sponsors of contests notify their winners by mail, so be very careful.

- Do not answer telephone survey questions. Request the caller to send you a written questionnaire by mail.
- Never allow children to play with the phone. It is not a toy. It could lead to dialing someone's number and irritating them. It could possibly be the phone of an elderly person who has trouble getting to it, not to mention a surprise on your phone bill if they happen to reach a long distance number.
- Never allow children to answer the phone. They are quick to provide sensitive information to a caller, such as, "My mommy and daddy are not home. I live at 1234 Tree Street."
- All responsible children should be taught to understand and respect the telephone, and how to dial the police and fire department. It is also good for them to know their own phone number. Test them.
- Do not tie up the phone for long periods of time.
- Report trouble with your phone immediately. After all, most of us pay for the right to use the phone, so it should be in good working order.
- If a telephone repairman arrives, check to see if you can see his truck or van. Does he have his tools? Can he identify himself? Call the phone company when possible to confirm his story.

Obscene Phone Calls

- Hang up immediately on obscene phone callers. Do not engage in conversation or shouting matches. This is what they want.
- Report all crank or obscene phone calls to the police and the telephone company. After a while, if enough complaints stack up, they may decide to attempt to "trap" the caller while on the phone.
- If you receive a "heavy breather" or obscene caller, hang up. If he continues, blow a loud shrieking, high pitched

whistle or air horn into the phone, which should get your message across.

- If he continues, tell him the police have been notified and are monitoring the line.
- If necessary, change your phone number.

Strangers at your Door

Never, under any circumstances, allow a stranger access to your house. Always determine what he wants, and confirm his story, if possible. What good are expensive locks and alarm systems if someone can walk into your home simply by asking permission? A large number of rapes and robberies begin with a courteous smile and a polite hello. People are easily fooled, and once the visitor is inside, the victim sees just how foolish he or she really was. Many times a criminal "cases" his potential target by gaining entrance under false pretenses.

Keep the criminal outside:

- Never allow a stranger into your home. If he asks to use the phone to call a tow truck, inform him you will make the call for him.
- Teach young children never to answer the door.
- Never admit maintenance personnel without first confirming who they are. A few seconds will not mess up the schedule. If you never called them, get the name, full identification, vehicle description, and license number. Then call the business to confirm why they are there. If no adequate answer is given, call the police.
- Never leave a stranger alone with your children or alone in any room.
- Inform servants not to let a stranger in until identification is confirmed.
- Always observe visitors through a peephole or window.
- Never open the door to strangers without using the safety chain, and hold at least one foot securely against the base of the door.
- Report all suspicious activity and strange vehicles to police immediately.
- Ask sales people to leave brochures in the mail box or by the foot of the door.

Reporting a Crime or Suspicious Activity

Many crimes could be stopped if people would just pick up the phone and call the police. It's not a requirement to provide your name if you feel uncomfortable about it. The important thing is to report the crime. People in this country have got to get involved if we are ever to stand a chance of beating crime.

Be Aware of Suspicious Behavior

Take note of any activity not considered normal, such as:
- A stranger closely observing a home or car.
- Someone attempting to enter a home or car using force, or having difficulty in obtaining entrance.
- Anyone standing in or around buses, or behind objects, attempting to conceal himself.
- Someone running from a home.
- Someone screaming.
- A moving van with workers loading furniture from a home when you doubt that the residents are present or that they intend to move.
- A stranger talking with or offering candy or rides to children.
- Someone who dresses and acts in ways that are inappropriate to the neighborhood or the weather.
- A stranger parked in a car closely observing people and residences.
- Someone peeking in windows.
- A vehicle that repeatedly drives slowly through your neighborhood.
- Someone who knocks on the front door or rings the doorbell and then goes around to the rear of the house.
- An abandoned vehicle.

Obtain a Good Description

Providing the police with an accurate description of a stranger or criminal can in many cases be the key to a quick and effective arrest. Always observe the situation and record the following:
- Sex of the individual
- Height

- Weight
- Race
- Clothes—color, style, accessories (hat, jewelry, etc.), type of footwear
- Hair color, length, style, including facial hair
- Eye color, shape; eyeglasses
- Physical build
- Physical deformities
- Verbal/speech patterns
- Any conversation or names you overhear

Vehicles

- License number, state
- Type of vehicle (car, truck, motorcycle, van, etc.)
- Color
- Make, model
- Year
- Two-door or four-door
- Visible damage
- Extras (e.g., CB antenna, ski rack)
- Time and direction of travel
- How many occupants

How To Report the Crime

Always call the police immediately upon suspecting suspicious activity. It's better to be a little embarrassed if nothing is wrong than to let a criminal escape. Remember:

- Time is very important. Report the crime immediately.
- Always remain calm and collected.
- Provide the police with your name, address, and phone number.
- Provide the police with the address of the suspicious activity.
- Provide the police information as to what the suspicious activity is.
- Provide the police a complete description of the suspect and of any vehicle involved.

What To Do When Surprised by an Intruder

Everyone has at some time worried about the possibility that they or a member of their family will be home when a criminal decides to force his way in. What should a person do in this kind of situation?

When an intruder demands your money and jewelry, always obey him. Any half-planned struggle or resistance on your part may get you or another family member hurt. As in all threatening situations, resistance should be used only as a last resort. Remain calm and allow the burglar to escape uncontested. Above all, never attempt to chase after him. Call the police and provide an accurate report of the incident and description of the criminal. Next, determine where and how the intruder managed to enter without being heard or seen, and take whatever measures are necessary to prevent another unexpected visit. If your home had been properly secured, with adequate locks and lighting, most intruders would not have been able to forcefully enter without being heard. Unfortunately, many times the burglar simply walks through an unlocked back door or crawls through an open window.

Okay, let's assume you have taken every precautionary measure possible to ward off an intruder, and one still tries to force his way in. What now? Several actions can be taken, provided each action is safe, practical, and based on common sense. To start with, let's say that one night you suspect that someone is attempting to force open your back door. A quick look through the back window confirms your suspicions. First, call the police, then turn on every light possible to try to frighten him off. Gather up family members and exit through the front door, running to a neighbor for help. If for some reason you cannot escape immediately and safely, retreat to your security room if you have one. If your only other alternative is to sit tight and wait for help, find a spot in your house that offers concealment while, if possible, providing observation of the area the intruder is trying to enter. Grab a weapon like a ball bat, golf club, fireplace poker, or knife, and yell a warning to the burglar. Let him know that you have called the police (even if for some reason you were unable to), and inform him you have a weapon and will use it if he continues. You might even consider barking ferociously like a killer dog. Sounds silly, but anything that will cause the intruder to have second thoughts is worth the effort! Actually, any intelligent criminal, (or I should say, any criminal with average intelligence), is going to run as soon as you hit the lights. If the intruder's activity appears to stop, continue to expect the unexpected. He could be waiting for you to open a door or window to check out the situation, which will make it easier for him to attack. Remain alert and calm and still be sure to call the police to report the incident. They should place a patrol in the area to watch for further suspicious activity.

Most criminals want to remain unseen and unheard. But what about the one who is under the influence of drugs or alcohol, or possibly mentally disturbed? Since he cannot think rationally, rational actions to scare him off may not work. These criminals are very, very dangerous and will quite possibly attack you because you are in their way. You must avoid them at all costs.

What about the intruder who, fearing nothing, rips the door off its hinges and continues advancing? At this point it is obvious that you have provided ample warning. Now it's either submit totally and hope for mercy, or stand and fight. Given enough time to prepare and the proper attitude, the homeowner can, in most cases, drop the intruder where he stands. This is accomplished by obtaining a weapon and taking a position affording the advantage of surprise. If armed with a firearm, shoot a warning shot (if you have enough time) into a solid piece of furniture. This should keep the bullet from penetrating a wall and striking an innocent person. It should convince him to turn and run, but if not, you may have to shoot him. At this time don't concern yourself with legalities. If the incident happened as described here, the use of deadly force would probably be justified since you feared bodily harm or death. If you are armed with a club or knife, your initial attack must be forceful and accurate. Use whatever force is necessary to stop the criminal. Once you overpower the assailant, make sure he is totally unable to retaliate. Tie him up or stand guard over him with a weapon until help arrives. Never render first aid if there is a chance that he may grab you and continue his plans. Do so only when you are 100 percent positive that you can provide aid without endangering yourself or another family member. Remember, this guy is probably desperate and would take whatever measure necessary to overpower you and escape. If possible, call for an ambulance.

Awakened By An Intruder?

What should you do when you wake up and realize an intruder is already prowling around inside your home? Usually the best approach is to stay in bed and pretend to be asleep until you can escape, lock your door, or call the police. It's possible the burglar won't even see you, if he does, chances are he will leave or continue quietly before exiting. In some cases, if the intruder has other plans (assault or rape) you better be prepared either to consent or to resist. You may be better off submitting to all demands. This does not mean you chose to be assaulted, but that you had no other way to insure your safety or the safety of the child in the next room.

If you decide to resist, do so intelligently. Take advantage of the element of surprise, which is on your side. Secure a weapon (knife, club, firearm), possibly concealed under your mattress, and wait to see if he will enter and approach you. Don't make any sudden moves until he is directly over you. It is possible that he may enter your room only to search for valuables, then quietly exit. Any quick act on your part here could prove fatal to you, unless you are absolutely sure of success. If he decides to wake you or physically assault you, he probably will get within arm's reach to check you out. Let him get as close as possible, then let him have it with all you've got until you are sure you are safe. Always remember you are taking the chance that this could backfire on you. He could take any weapon you have away and use it against you. This decision is strictly up to you, based on the circumstances at hand.

It is very important for each family to establish some form of defensive plan against intruders. It is also a good idea to teach household employees and babysitters how to react to this threat.

Listing and Marking Your Valuables

Two important ways to cut your losses in case of theft or fire are to maintain an updated inventory of your property and to mark all valuables with a registration identification number.

By keeping an accurate list of your property (including stocks, bonds, and securities), you will know when something is missing. In case of fire, you can immediately supply your insurance agent with this list. In case of burglary, you can quickly pinpoint the missing items and notify the police immediately. The sooner the theft is reported, the better your chance to regain your property if it is located.

The best way to identify your property is to mark it with a special code (social security number, state abbreviation, drivers license number, etc.). This can be done with an engraving tool or with invisible marking techniques such as the ultraviolet pen, which only reveals the marking when placed under ultraviolet light. Since it's invisible, it prevents the thief from sanding off your identification number.

Your inventory list should include a detailed description of each item, with serial numbers or identification numbers, value of item, when purchased, and, if possible, a copy of the sales receipt (Figure 2-11). It's very important to supply your insurance agent with a complete copy of your inventory list, and to update it periodically. It's also wise to keep an additional copy in a safe deposit box or with a trusted relative. Another safety technique: photographic records of your valuables, especially high-value items like jewelry, coins, art, and antiques.

Whenever a robbery or larceny is committed and reported to the police, any identification on stolen objects is logged into the National Crime Information Center (NCIC) computer. When items are returned or recovered, the computer is searched by using available serial numbers or other recorded identification, and the property can be returned if claimed.

Marked property is frowned upon by burglars because it can quickly be traced. Thus, by applying warning stickers to your doors (back and front) and windows, you can help deter burglary. Most police departments will help you mark your valuables and can also provide warning stickers.

Figure 2-11
Inventory List

Name: _____

Address: _____

City: _____ **State:** _____ **Zip:** _____

Phone Number: _____

Insurance Company: _____

Address: _____

Phone Number: _____

Claim Number: _____

Date of Inventory: _____ **Updated On:** _____

ROOM	ITEM ID / SERIAL #	VALUE	DATE OF PUR.	MISC. DATA

Records of Stocks, Bonds, and Insurance Policies

TYPE OF SECURITY	VALUE AMOUNT	POLICY NUMBER

Hiring Household Staff

Anyone who enjoys the same freedoms within a home as the family members (babysitters, maids, butlers), should be completely honest and trustworthy. Unfortunately, the days of unlocked doors and unquestioned friendships are coming to an end. How often do we read about the babysitter or housekeeper who assaulted, kidnapped, or killed a little child in their care? It is extremely important to thoroughly evaluate prospective household employees. Expect the same qualities and concerns from the housekeeper as from yourself. If they are uneducated about family protection, teach them. Your family's safety is at stake.

Every employee should be subject to a police records check, at the very minimum. Anyone who shies away from this request could have something to hide. If they should say, "So I made one mistake, it won't happen again," don't base your family's well-being on whether this person has reformed. It also depends on what type of record a person might have. Although an extensive history of driving violations does not mean this person is irresponsible, arrests for drunk driving would be grounds for disqualifying them for a position that requires child care or supervision. A record that shows a petty theft charge during high school ten years ago, however, does not necessarily mean the applicant should be disqualified. You must use common sense and consider the time period involved. People do grow up and mature. We all have weaknesses, but be sure the weaknesses your employees have cannot harm your family. An example of a household staff profile is found in Figure 2-12.

Figure 2-12
Staff Background Data

Staff Position: _____

Full Name/Alias: _____

Date/Place of Birth: _____

Address: _____

Home Phone: _____

Prior Employment: _____

Address: _____ Phone: _____

Former Supervisor: _____

References: _____

Special Qualifications *(First Aid, CPR, Nurse, Bodyguard, etc.):* _____

_____

Misc. Data: * _____

_____

Local Agency Checks:

☐ Local Police Results _____

☐ Local Court (if necessary) _____

_____

Signature of Staff Member

_____

Date

OPTION: Include statement informing applicant of possible polygraph examination prior to and during employment.

Additional skills, such as first aid training, CPR, or registered nurse are an obvious plus. Anyone who demonstrates an interest in safety and security should be strongly considered.

Don't feel obligated to hire friends and relatives for these positions. Most people hesitate to express their true feelings to them simply because they are friends or relatives. You must be able to establish guidelines and enforce them rigorously.

Babysitters should be mature enough to understand and carry out your instructions completely. They must be able to handle situations that may require difficult decisions, including precautions against burglars. Do not assume they can handle all situations. Question them and run them through a series of practical tests to see what they know and how well they react to pressure. This may sound a little overboard, but that's because few people are really serious when it comes to family protection. By all means, forbid the babysitter to have guests, especially a girlfriend or boyfriend. The *first* time orders are disobeyed, fire him or her. That first time could have cost the life of your child.

All attention must be given to the job at hand to insure adequate responses to an unexpected emergency. Emphasis must be on prevention. Maids, butlers, housekeepers, and maintenance personnel must be fully aware of family security procedures and follow them to the letter.

When household staff members understand their instructions, they will usually comply. Work toward developing a family relationship whenever possible; staff personnel are more aware and responsible when they feel it's more than just a job.

When you are away for a night or longer, always tell the housekeeper or babysitter exactly where you will be. I recommend a bulletin board that displays specific instructions, including your location, phone number, when you intend to return, and any special medicine to be administered to children. Your address should be prominently displayed so that in case of an emergency it can be relayed properly to authorities (Figure 2-13). Keep a Family Data File (Figure 2-14) on each family member and make it accessible to staff personnel in case of an emergency.

Figure 2-13
For Family Bulletin Board

Family's Name: _____

Address: _____

Phone Number: _____

We are at: _____ **Phone Number:** _____

We will be back at: _____

In case of emergency contact: _____

At Phone Number: _____

Police: _____ **Fire:** _____

Hospital: _____ **Poison Control:** _____

Doctor's Name/Number: _____

Special Instructions: _____

_____

Figure 2-14
Emergency Information
Family Data File

Name: _____

Date/Place of Birth: _____

Age: _____ **Sex:** _____ **Blood Type:** _____

Special Medications: _____

Allergies/Reactions: _____

_____

Special Instructions: _____

_____

Doctor's Name/Number: _____

Religion: _____

NOTE: Complete for each member of the family.

Rural Crime

More than eight million crimes occur each year in rural areas. This is partly because large quantities of farm equipment and other valuable items are inadequately protected, including farm animals that are not properly marked or branded for identification.

Equipment

To help fight crime on the farm, you must establish a program of crime prevention. As essential steps in your program, you should:

- Light all areas of the farm.
- Place locks on storage sheds, feed and grain elevators, gas pumps, and farm tools such as plows, discs, etc. These should be chained to a permanent fixture.
- Never leave large equipment in the fields at night. Lock them in a barn or shed or to a permanent fixture that is well-lighted.
- Use alarm systems if possible on all vehicles, or at a minimum, include a "kill-switch" to keep ignition from starting.
- Inventory and mark all equipment with social security number and state. Place markings in two locations, the first in a visible area. The second should be in a concealed, secret location, so that if the first marking is sanded off or painted over, you can still identify it. Also take photographs of all your large, more valuable equipment, giving copies to your insurance agent.

CHAPTER THREE

Establishing A Neighborhood Watch Program

Throughout the United States today, more and more concerned citizens are volunteering their time to help fight crime in their communities. The best way to do this is to volunteer your assistance in a neighborhood watch program, crime-stoppers association, or other program organized by a civic or church group in cooperation with the local police department. There are many benefits to programs of this nature, but the true goal of a neighborhood watch program is the protection of life and property.

Once established, the neighborhood watch program helps close the communication gap between neighbors, the community, and the police. This allows for a greater understanding of each other, in addition to providing the perfect opportunity for better police/community relations. Trust and community pride grow as police and community involvement grows. Not only are the police and the citizens drawn together in a common cause, the people themselves begin to open up and communicate with their neighbors, many for the first time. The end result is a community that effectively works together to reduce crime.

How to Get Started

An interest in forming a neighborhood watch program can be generated by a citizen, a school, or a civic or church group coordinating with the local police department. Most police departments welcome any organized and controlled assistance they can get.

The community must be educated about the causes and effects of crime, as well as how to plan prevention. Once a sincere interest begins to grow, there should be a meeting (usually organized by the police department) where the neighborhood watch program proposal is discussed and the specific areas of concern identified.

What is Required

The neighborhood watch program's primary function is to observe and report suspicious/illegal activity. The emphasis is on reporting crime, not engaging it. Let common sense be your guide. The community as a whole can provide much better visual observation than any police department, no matter how large, simply because there are more citizens than officers.

For the first step, a police representative is usually assigned to assist the neighborhood in establishing its neighborhood watch program. This representative will normally contact key individuals to organize a community meeting. Included in this meeting should be the mayor, councilmen, businessmen, and any other interested citizens of the community. It is best to hold this type of meeting at a location that can handle a large crowd.

During the meeting, the police representative should discuss the proposal, give a crime prevention presentation and/or show a movie about establishing a neighborhood watch program.

Once the major details are discussed and understood, the citizens should select a neighborhood watch chairman and individual block captains to supervise the program, in addition to a neighborhood watch committee. Once the committee is established, the organization by-laws should be tentatively written, to include such articles as:

- Designation and purpose of the program
- Membership
- Rights and privileges
- Officers

- Duties of officers
- Methods of elections
- Amendments

Monthly meetings (at the town hall or church basement) should be scheduled for block captains, always including the police department representative. An annual membership meeting should be held to re-elect new officers and introduce new members. Be certain to get adequate media coverage to advertise this new program to other interested citizens. This also serves to warn criminals that from now on the citizens will be watching and reporting any suspicious activities or individual(s).

Establish neighborhood watch rosters and charts that clearly identify all the neighborhood boundaries, member names, phone numbers, addresses, etc. Be sure that permission is received prior to distribution of personal information to other members. The neighborhood watch captain, his committee, and police should get a copy of the total breakdown of the neighborhood.

Prepare literature that describes techniques of crime prevention. Design and print up decals and stickers.

Establish guidelines on how to observe suspicious activity, how to obtain a good description of an incident, and how to report it to the police. Familiarize each member with surrounding homes, addresses and phone numbers, to aid in speedy reporting of suspicious activity (Figure 3-1). Insist that all activity be written down and kept by the neighborhood watch chairman for future use.

Your neighborhood watch program should become involved in establishing crime-prevention techniques and performing security surveys. Other valuable programs can also be implemented, such as:

- The inventory and marking of valuables to be recorded and placed in a secure file at the police department
- Assistance for senior citizens
- Child safety and identification programs
- Courses in defensive tactics
- Establishing a crime prevention month
- Establishing a volunteer program designed to allow authorized civilians to assist the local police in crime prevention.

Figure 3-1
Alert Roster
Neighborhood Watchers Reporting Procedures:

Watcher (Emergency) ⟶ **Police Department** ⟶ **Block Captain**

Watcher (Non-Emergency) ⟶ **Block Captain** ⟶ **Neighborhood**

Watch Chairman ⟶ **Police**

When reporting an emergency, notify your local police immediately, then block captain. When reporting a non-emergency, contact your block captain who contacts the neighborhood watch chairman who should make the appropriate reports for future use.

Neighborhood Watchers should be able to identify each of their neighbors' residences and maintain the appropriate addresses and phone numbers to inform police in the event of an emergency.

Watcher's Name: _____

Address: _____ **Phone Number:** _____

Police Phone Number: _____ **Fire Phone Number:** _____

Hospital/Rescue Phone Number: _____

Block Captain's Name: _____

Address: _____ **Phone Number:** _____

NOTE: Block Captain should have Watch Chairman listed on his/her chart.

Activity Spotted: _____

Location: _____ **Date:** _____ **Time:** _____

Descriptions of Persons/Vehicles: _____

It's important for each community to use its resources to the fullest. Tackle one or two specific crime problems at a time, and watch the program grow in size and accomplishments. Don't try to attack every possible problem in the community at the same time, or you will find the committees overburdened and spread too thin to be of any real assistance.

Ingredients of a Strong Program

1. Be sure all members are residents of the neighborhood. It would, to say the least, be counter-productive for crooks to join your organization!

2. Try not to schedule too much work or too many meetings for volunteers. Remember, they have their families to take care of first.

3. Take time to become established and operational.

4. Include all areas of crime prevention.

5. Don't overstep bounds and interfere with others' rights by believing you are now a police representative and have authority to enforce laws. You will only create hard feelings among the community and give the neighborhood watch program a bad name.

CHAPTER 4

Man's Best Friend: A Pooch for Protection

If a little extra security and companionship is desired, consider getting a pooch for protection. Whether you acquire a professionally trained guard dog or find a lovable mutt at the pound, dogs can effectively deter crime.

For many years dogs have been used to guard property and lives, to search out contraband, to track down criminals and lost children, and to guide the blind. The services a dog can provide seem endless, not to mention the love and loyalty they show for their owners.

Although not all pets are going to jump between you and a potential mugger, an obedient canine can provide you with an invaluable psychological advantage over a criminal. Many dogs have been known to give their lives for their masters. Few sane people will take the chance of entering your property or attacking your person when it's obvious a dog is present.

Short, tall, fat, or skinny, a dog can scare the daylights out of just about anyone not familiar with its abilities. A dog in the home or roving on the property will, in most cases, keep a criminal away. Since time and concealment are the most important factors to a thief, if they are confronted with a barking dog or find themselves staring at a dog between them and their target, they will probably think twice and seek a more secluded, less noisy, and "safer" home to enter. If, while a criminal attempts to break into a residence, he sees or hears a dog yapping away inside, his intentions may change. Not only is a barking dog a roving alarm system, it also may prove to be a dangerous emissary. Why risk it? As long as this is the philosophy of a criminal, the dog, professionally trained or not, will remain invaluable!

Do you need a professionally trained guard or attack dog, or will the average house pet be sufficient? Experts in this field have varied opinions regarding trained guard dogs.

Professional guard or attack dogs are generally trained by experts in this field, but some authorities say you can train your own dog under the supervision of an expert trainer.

Guard and attack dogs are trained primarily to react very aggressively to any and all situations pertaining to their duties. Their main goal is to guard, deter, or engage an intruder. Because they are trained to react so aggressively, these dogs should not be taken home as family pets. Most professional dogs of this nature are kept in pens, awaiting their tour of duty, and do not reside with the average family, enjoying the relaxed life of another family member. Some experts do say that a professional guard or attack dog can leave its job and then be taken home among the family, without fear of injury to children or adults.

Professional dogs are trained to obey specific commands. These commands can be conveyed verbally, or with hand movements, or by using both methods, depending on training. These dogs are usually obedient to only one master. What about the family member who startles or accidentally signals the dog to attack? Or is the possibility that this would happen very small because such animals obey only their master's commands?

These coments raise questions in many minds. "If professional trainers disagree, should I risk my family's safety by exposing them to a professional guard/attack dog as a pet?" I am neither in favor of nor against bringing a guard dog, professionally trained or otherwise, into your home. My interest is only to *alert* you to the possible dangers involved when exposed to any animal trained to be aggressive.

After all, there have been occasions when so-called family pets have killed their owners, so to condemn professional dogs is hardly fair. I have personally worked with professional guard and attack dogs and felt comfortable petting and playing with them. I have also worked with those who would just as soon take your arm off as look at you.

It all boils down to how well the animal is trained, what conditions it is exposed to, and how much affection is provided. Be aware that there are many so-called professional trainers and professionally trained dogs that are phonies. Because there is a lot of money to be made by training and selling professional guard and attack dogs, the business attracts many unscrupulous people out to make a fast buck.

If you are seriously considering purchasing a professional dog for security reasons, then snoop around and get one that's fully qualified. Take the time to ask other dog owners which trainers they would recommend, and which ones you should avoid. Check your phone directory for ones near you, but visit more than one to be safe. Ask yourself, "How long has this trainer been around? Has anybody heard of him, or purchased one of his animals? What sort of track record do the trainer and his dogs have?" Check with your local kennel association, protective league, dog pound, and/or police. If the trainer is a traveling salesperson, I would stay away from him. Once you visit a trainer, have him thoroughly run the dog through his commands. It is important that the trainer can effectively control the dog, and be sure to test how quickly the animal obeys the command to cease its attack! It's just as important that he be able to respond to your commands! Make sure the animal has its required shots and is healthy. Any dog that shows signs of beatings, or appears sickly, may have been mistreated and is a time bomb just waiting to explode.

After you purchase your dog, or even if you rent one from an owner to patrol your business, remember you are responsible and liable for its actions. Proper barriers must be constructed and warning signs posted to keep the animal from accidentally escaping and attacking an innocent victim. Since this dog's primary role is to protect and he is capable of aggressiveness, be sure to provide the necessary safeguards to prevent an accidental injury. Professional guard and attack dogs have been and will continue to be irreplaceable. Their actions have protected an indeterminable amount of property, but most importantly, they have guarded and saved lives.

If you decide that this is the protection you need, then feel comfortable in the knowledge that these animals perform, probably in most cases, with more courage and instinct than that of a human.

Now, let's talk about the average house dog found across the country. Does he have to be big, or bark ferociously? No, he doesn't. With the exception of the determined professional, the mere presence of a dog in most cases will keep a person from entering your residence. (If the professional intends to break in, he will be prepared. He will either drug your dog, maneuver his attention elsewhere, or possibly even shoot him.)

Is There a "Best" Breed?

For a family, the "best" dog will be the one that provides the most love and affection. Of course, size has advantages and disadvantages. If you live in a small apartment, a large German Shepherd would be impractical, but a tiny Chihuahua can provide affection and bark its little head off at the first indication of an intruder. If you live on a large ranch or farm, then several midsize to large dogs may be your answer. They have room to run and can effectively deter trespassers over a large territory.

I would not give up one dog for another because he doesn't seem to be the courageous protector you had hoped. All dogs develop a sense of loyalty, and establish their boundaries or domain. When tested, they will at least appear to stand their ground. Remember, the stranger does not know what actions your dog will take. When approached by a suspicious-looking stranger, just attach a leash to your pet (even if you know that Spot is not going anywhere and he just stares at you in confusion), and warn the intruder to depart. If necessary, act like you are about to unleash a terrible killer upon him. Once he leaves, you both can go back inside and have a good laugh and a milkbone.

How Do Dogs React?

As a rule, when a dog is approached, he will react in one of the following ways:

1. He will run up to you, wag his tail, sniff the various scents on your clothes, and try to jump all over you, wanting you to pet him. A pushover, this dog will make friends with everyone and anyone.
2. He will stand his ground, barking, or remain silent. This is the one that you cannot be sure of. He could attack or run away.

3. This one, at the first sign of company, will run and hide with his tail between his legs, usually tossing a bark or two at you from behind the couch or from behind the legs of his owner. He is not really a direct physical threat—his bark really is worse than his bite!

4. Then there is the one who immediately springs to meet you—growling, snarling, and possibly snapping, daring you to move another inch. Whatever you do, don't turn and run. Freeze and wait for help. This one is likely to draw blood.

CHAPTER FIVE

Recognizing Threats In The Work Environment

The buses were running late that morning—six inches of new snow had fallen the night before. Sarah was worried that she would be late for a meeting—she *had* to get to work on time so she opted for the warmer, drier, unfamiliar subway. In her hurry, Sarah didn't notice the teenager sneaking up on her and stared in amazement as he ran off with her shoulder bag into the rush-hour traffic.

From the day we receive our social security card to the day we retire, our lives are shaped and guided by our ability to earn a living. Very few Americans can choose not to work. Most of us must get up and go out into the world to earn a paycheck. This daily ritual can become so routine that we find ourselves taking for granted ordinary actions like walking to the car or waiting for a bus. With our thoughts elsewhere, we often forget, for example, to check the inside of the car before we get in. This simple but very important act might someday save your life. So, as in the chapter on home environments, we must carefully and thoroughly examine the areas of danger that may threaten us when we leave home and venture out into the "jungle."

Leaving Home

Before you leave home be sure that you have locked all your doors and windows. Make sure all appliances (stove, iron, coffee maker) are turned off or unplugged to prevent accidents. Double-check the front door on the way out, and by all means leave a light on if you intend to return home after nightfall.

Personal Transportation

The threat of an attack in your own home is relatively small compared to the threat facing individuals who live in apartments or homes that require parking in public lots or on the street. If possible, lock your vehicle inside a secure garage. If you must park outside or in an indoor parking lot, opt for a spot that is not secluded. If you live in an apartment complex with indoor public parking, I suggest you get together with the other tenants and request proper lighting and the installation of an alarm system. If you are really persuasive, the landlord may hire a guard to watch the premises. Unfortunately, it may take a crime or series of crimes before a landlord listens. At the minimum, create a buddy system where two of you meet at a designated time and proceed to your cars together. It's harder to rendezvous for a return trip, so try to leave during daylight hours or get a friend to accompany you if you must leave later. You may be able to call ahead before leaving work and have a friend or relative meet you. When possible, car-pool with members of your apartment complex, which is a very economical and safe way to travel to and from work.

Before getting in a vehicle, always take a good look inside to be sure no one is there. If the doors that you locked are unlocked, do not get inside. Return to your residence and call police, or at least ask a friend to check it out with you.

Once safely inside your vehicle, always lock your doors and roll windows up to a safe level. Keep a half-tank of fuel in the vehicle for safety's sake. In addition, every vehicle should carry these items:

- First-aid kit
- Blankets
- Spare tire (check periodically for condition)
- Tire-changing tools
- Fire extinguisher
- Flares or reflectors
- White flag or rag
- Appropriate repair tools

If you break down along the way to work, always pull off the road, out of the path of oncoming traffic. Pull into a driveway or business parking lot, if possible, to perform repairs. If you're along the road in an unfamiliar area and have no help immediately available, you should:

- Open the hood and raise it all the way.
- At night, place flares or reflectors approximately 40 feet in front of and behind the vehicle.
- Tie a white flag on the door of the driver's side or the car's radio or CB antenna.
- Remain in the vehicle with the doors locked.
- Keep the vehicle in park and engine "off," if possible, to prevent the possibility of carbon monoxide poisoning. Remember—carbon monoxide is not always identifiable by its smell. It usually enters your system undetected, causing unconsciousness, then death.
- If changing a tire, always block the front tires when jacking up the rear, and block the rear tires and apply the emergency brake when jacking up the front. Don't accidentally lock your keys in the trunk or inside the car or you will be in even worse shape.
- If another motorist stops to help, you must judge whether to accept it or not. It is usually recommended that you roll your window down, ask the motorist to call for a service truck or family member, or wait for a police car to arrive. They can request help for you.
- If, while you are driving to work, another driver begins to harass you with his vehicle, attempts to get you to stop, or tries to force you off the road, keep driving until you can find help. Never stop to argue with a person like this. Write down their license number and a description of the vehicle and driver, then notify the police.
- Never pick up hitchhikers.

Public Transportation

Every day thousands rely on the public transportation system to get them to and from work. This is especially true in or near large cities such as New York, Cleveland, and Boston. Although most public systems provide police or security services, many do not. Even where police security services are available, they are usually spread out over a large area, making immediate response to an illegal activity difficult or impossible. The best thing you can do for protection is to be aware of the people and the activities around you.

On buses, you are fairly safe since there usually are many riders. When waiting for a bus, remain alert for potential purse snatchers or muggers. Stay with the general crowd and secure all packages tightly. *Never* leave a bag or package unattended. Do not exit a bus in an unfamiliar area. If you are lost, ask the driver for help or remain on the bus until it arrives in a familiar locale or returns to its terminal.

Seat yourself as close to the front as possible, and watch for pickpockets. On a crowded bus, a pickpocket can have a field day with unsuspecting riders. Keep all bags and briefcases in plain sight—on your lap if at all possible. As you get off the bus, be alert for purse-snatchers and muggers waiting to nab you as you step off the bus.

In taxis, make sure you have flagged down a legitimate taxi service. Unfamiliar or suspicious-looking vehicles should never be entered. Once inside a taxi, make sure the usual items found inside (meter, maps, charts, change box) are present, or get out immediately. Provide clear instructions, and if the driver deviates from them, create an excuse to stop. Get out, and notify police and taxi headquarters. Make sure to obtain the license number, taxi number, and description of the vehicle and driver. (Think how easy it would be to fix up a car to look like a local taxi and abduct or rob potential customers!)

Subways and trains have both underground threats and aboveground threats. Plan accordingly. Know where the driver and security guards are located and move to that locale if possible. When in doubt, exit the train. Never stay in an area that could be dangerous, especially an unlighted car that's empty.

When traveling by air, always comply with all rules and regulations of the carrier. Plan your travel arrangements completely, and always confirm scheduled flights. Leave a copy of your itinerary with someone. Lock all baggage and mark all pieces with your complete address and phone number. Remove flight tags from previous trips to prevent an accidental misrouting of your luggage. I recommend that you always keep hand-carried items with you while waiting for your flight, and not lock them in airport lockers. Lockers are generally easily broken into, and sometimes more than one key exists to open them. If childen are accompanying you, never allow them out of your sight. Most airports (all U.S. airports) provide a high degree of security and the chances of trouble are slim.

Once you arrive at your destination by personal or public means, attempt to get as close to your work site as possible. If you are parking a vehicle, always park in a visible, well lighted location, with windows up and keys in your possession before locking the doors. Walk with others when possible, especially at night, with your keys firmly in your hand to help defend against a possible mugger.

If you must park underground or in a secluded parking lot, try not to be alone. Never leave your keys with the attendant, and lock valuables in your trunk. These are very dangerous locations so obtain an escort if at all possible, especially at night.

Walk confidently, with a positive attitude. Hold your purse and/or briefcase securely in the hand that faces the street. Again, it's a good idea to have your keys ready in case of an attack. It's also a good idea to carry an umbrella or cane to and from your car, even if rain is not predicted. They can be formidable weapons if you are attacked. You may want to carry a whistle or compressed-air horn to blow if attacked. Your best defense, if approached, is to scream.

Once inside the building where you work, go directly to your destination. Don't assume that you are now completely safe from threats.

Ride elevators only when more than one person is aboard with you, and then hope that they are not partners in crime. If you feel uneasy with them, listen to your instincts and exit immediately. When riding the elevator, know where all the operation buttons are and what they do, especially the emergency "STOP" button. If attacked, you can push this button. Most elevators are equipped with intercom systems that are used for communication when the emergency stop button is pushed. So if you push it, yell for help. Try to remain calm so you will remember to yell which way you are going, up or down, to alert the elevator monitors. When you are already on an elevator, stay alert but look confident and ready. If a strange person(s) enters, such as a drunk off the street, or a person apparently high on drugs, exit immediately. Don't place yourself in jeopardy. In many cities, street people and derelicts enter public buildings to get out of the cold or rain. They usually spend time riding the elevators or visiting the restrooms. I don't mean to say that everyone coming in out of the rain and cold is dangerous, but that the possibility of a lonely desperate person turning to crime is real, and he may come inside to commit it.

In addition, never walk up or down stairways alone. This is a prime sector for illegal activity.

When entering public restroom facilities, be aware of individuals inside. This is another location where criminals can attack. If necessary, leave and come back later, or go to another restroom.

When you leave work for lunch, to shop, or to return home, be sure to practice all security measures. Once home, make sure it's safe to get out of your car. If you're in a parking garage and see strange individuals, drive out and contact police immediately. If you are unable to exit safely, honk your horn, continually. This should get rid of any suspicious characters and at the same time draw attention to you. Remain in your locked car until someone arrives to escort you or until you feel it's safe to exit. Don't forget, it's a good idea to carry your keys firmly in your strong hand to help defend against an assailant. When taking a taxi home, you can always ask the driver to wait until you have unlocked your door and entered. If you notice an open window or unlocked door, or any suspicious vehicle or person outside your residence, contact the police immediately.

Starting A New Job

When arriving in a new area for the first time, carefully study the environment during nights and weekends to get an idea of activities during these times. In addition, ask to review the company's security policies. If none exist, recommend that some be developed and implemented. Examples of items that should be included:

- Every business should have personnel data on all employees and their families that includes emergency information. They should be reviewed and updated periodically.
- Personnel records should be secured.
- Nobody but authorized personnel should have access to them.

- Family members should be able to contact you in the event of an emergency. Provide them with complete written instructions.

Occupations and Their Hazards

Since much of today's crime takes place in the "white collar" business section (banks, drugstores, 24-hour convenience stores), let's look closely at several occupations that have continually been targeted by criminals. Their examples will help others devise step-by-step strategies to deter and counter threats.

Although the conditions cited may in some instances seem extreme, each of them reflects the reality of today's threats.

The Executive

The traditional pressures associated with executive-level jobs have been compounded in recent years by a new concern—the possibility of kidnapping or assassination. Many executives or members of their families have been victimized for economic or political reasons.

When a high-level corporate official is chosen as a kidnap victim, extortion is used for economic gain. The criminal has two main considerations in a case like this: safety, and money. In the few kidnapping cases that occur in the United States, the kidnapper rarely risks his life for the ransom. The terrorist, on the other hand, is out to gain attention for his cause. Most are highly trained and would readily die for their cause, or blow up a bus load of innocent people. Life for them, has less value than death in the line of "duty."

The executive whose international firm is located in one of the world's "hot spots," such as South America, is less concerned about whether criminals or terrorists have targeted him than by the fact that he may in fact be a target. It is vital that corporations design effective executive protection programs to prevent criminal and terrorist acts. Such programs are usually the responsibility of the firm's security department.

The executive's family is open to exploitation as well, and must be fully aware of the dimensions of these external threats. A complete executive protection plan should include procedures for all company employees and their families, and be practiced regularly, especially abroad.

The following recommendations identify key areas of concern.

Who qualifies as a target?

- Are you or your family wealthy?
- Are you an important executive of a large corporation?
- Does your firm have facilities overseas?
- Do you travel extensively?
- Do you travel overseas?
- Do you own stock in your firm?
- Do you serve on the board of directors of an international firm?
- Do you hold office or are you involved in any community organizations or projects?
- Would any person or organization stand to improve their position by kidnapping or murdering you?
- Have you or your corporation taken a political stance that is highly publicized, especially on foreign affairs?
- Has your corporation experienced labor disputes and/or been boycotted or picketed by organizations opposed to its activities?
- What is the state of the country your firm is located in? Is a political or military overthrow possible? If so, what might happen to you?
- Have you received any threats or experienced extortion in the past?

If most of your answers to these questions were yes, you must realistically consider yourself, or a member of your family or firm a potential target.

Prevention Policies

Here are some ideas to seriously consider:

- Develop codes between family members, servants, and company staff to use in warning each other in case of trouble. These codes must remain secret and be protected regularly (e.g., chauffeur verbally or visually signals executive of trouble).
- If possible, avoid public transportation systems.
- When traveling by air, always use United States carriers if possible.
- Never publicize your flight plans or itinerary.

- Allow only family or trusted associates to know schedules, etc.
- Never change flight schedules at the last minute without notifying appropriate personnel.
- Never make flight reservations by phone. Have someone pick them up for you, or arrive early and purchase prior to flight.
- When changing planes, or departing from a location, move confidently and quickly.
- Always avoid set patterns and routines. Change activities as necessary.
- Install alarm systems on all personal vehicles.
- Warn private staff/servants to be alert for unusual or strange activities.
- Chauffeurs should inspect vehicles daily, prior to operation, and double as bodyguards.
- Make sure that all vehicle hood latches are controlled from inside.
- Place a bolt through the tail pipe of all vehicles, to keep explosives from being placed inside.
- Train your chauffeur in defensive driving techniques.
- Keep corporate planes or boats under lock and key; install alarms; check daily.
- Park all vehicles indoors in a controlled, guarded location. Continual camera monitoring should be maintained.
- Never mark executive parking spots with names. Use a varying number system.
- Caution executive and family members not to advertise their location and vehicle by sporting a "personal" license plate that spells out their name or corporation. This goes for status symbols such as club memberships which could be used as identifiers.
- Install alarm systems for corporate buildings.
- Limit the number of access doors to business facilities.
- Remember that key control is critical.
- Control access to buildings and offices by using an effective pass and identification system.
- Escort all visitors.
- Install electronic remote lock switches to control access to sensitive areas from inside the area.

- Install bullet-resistant barriers at the reception area.
- Establish a code system for the receptionist and all other employees for notification in the event of an emergency (e.g., illegal attempt to enter facility).
- Escort hired janitorial/maintenance personnel to all locations.
- Lock all electrical/circuit boxes securely to prevent unauthorized entry.
- Closely monitor mail for letter bombs and potentially dangerous packages.
- Keep news releases about corporation activities and personnel brief, and *never* reveal sensitive plans or activities of the organization or its members and their families. Monitor financial and promotional news for unwanted disclosures.

Traveling Abroad

All foreign travel should be carefully planned, and passports and visas kept in order. It is essential to:

- Understand the customs and laws of the country you are visiting.
- Rent vehicles rather than draw attention to yourself with a corporate limousine.
- Know the language or have an interpreter with you.
- Know whom you are contacting.
- Know the location of the U.S. Embassy.
- Carry the currency of the country. (In many countries it is illegal to spend U.S. dollars.)

The Store Manager/Clerk

Most robberies occur just prior to the opening and closing of a business. It's prime time because few customers are around to witness or interfere with the criminal.

The businesses often marked as pushovers are small stores, including the many 24-hour operations scattered across the country. Not only are there few customers around, the manager or clerk is usually alone or aided by only one other employee. Too many of these stores fall victim to robberies for they qualify as "easy marks."

Some stores will always be more vulnerable to attack than others due to their location and clientele. For most, however, robbery attempts can be limited or deterred by effective security measures.

What Can an Owner/Manager Do?

- Provide proper lighting inside and out, especially behind the store. Darkness attracts and conceals criminals.
- Install adequate locks and alarms, and test their effectiveness regularly.
- Make sure that the parking lot and service areas (e.g., gas pumps) are well-lighted and can be clearly observed.
- Keep store windows free of advertisements to allow clear observation from outside by police or security patrols.
- Place the store safe in an open location that can be observed through front windows. (This deters criminals from break-ins.)
- Remove large quantities of cash and checks periodically and place them in a concealed safe for deposit at the bank at the first opportunity.
- Post signs that warn "No cash on hand after X p.m./a.m." or "After X p.m./a.m. no bills over $20.00 will be accepted."
- Never balance or exchange cash drawers in front of customers.
- Consider using a "dummy safe" which contains a convincing amount of cash and checks with actual funds secured elsewhere.
- Maintain serial numbers of large bills received.
- Establish a check-cashing policy and make sure that employees strictly adhere to it.
- Vary the route and carrier of bank deposits. Deposit during daylight hours.
- Set up an effective key-control system and check keys regularly.
- Install steel mesh or bars on windows, doors, and lights.
- Install bullet-proof/resistant barriers between office counters and customers.
- Keep high-value items out of windows to guard against criminals breaking the glass to grab the item.
- Install effective viewing mirrors, cameras, and one-way glass.
- Consider the use of a guard dog to patrol the premises after hours. Clearly post "Beware of Dog" warning signs.

- Establish an effective code system that allows employees to warn each other—both visibly and verbally—of trouble.

- Open and close the store with a minimum of two employees. One enters and turns off the alarm system and turns on the lights. Another waits outside, awaiting the signal that all is well. If the entering employee fails to show within an established time, the second employee calls the police. Reverse this policy when closing.

- If the store owner/manager receives a call to return to the store once it is closed, he should always notify another senior employee to meet him there and call the police to inform them of suspicious activity. Once inside, and prior to departure, if everything is okay, he should call the police within a set time period to tell them so. (This is good public relations. Never leave the police hanging and waiting.)

- Verify *all* calls received prior to departing for the store.

- Make sure that all employees understand that they should never argue or struggle with a troublemaker. Call police. They, or a customer, could be injured.

- Employees who are physically threatened or robbed should comply with all demands (use common sense), and cooperate fully if their lives are in danger. Never make any sudden moves. Remain calm and try to observe the criminal closely for a complete description of him and any weapon, if used.

- When accepting a "bad check," an "unauthorized credit card," or counterfeit money from a *known* problem customer, or from one threatening injury:

  1. Try to refuse tactfully, but accept if threatened.

  2. Let them depart from the store.

  3. Observe which vehicle they enter, record the vehicle description, license number, and the direction of departure.

  4. Record the criminal's description.

  5. Call the police immediately.

  6. Brief other employees to be on the look-out for the criminal.

The Drugstore Pharmacist

Your friendly neighborhood drugstore and the pharmacist who prepares your family prescriptions are rarely thought of by the average customer as targets of crime. Yet, approximately 90 percent of drugstore robberies committed each year occur in the pharmacy department. Armed robberies have doubled over previous years.

Drug theft for the purpose of sale or personal use is a growing problem throughout the United States. Thefts are committed both at night or early in the morning when nobody is around, and during business hours, putting the pharmacist's and customer's lives in jeopardy.

Rising illegal drug prices are forcing the drug user, who is running short of buying money, to walk into drugstores and take what he needs. The dealers and pushers find that it's often easier to acquire a new supply through the local pharmacist. Why pay to resupply their stock when they can simply walk into a store, put a gun to the pharmacist's head, and demand what they need? After all, there are thousands of pharmacy locations where you can purchase drugs. These drugstores offer virtually a never-ending supply of narcotics. Another common technique is to wait until the druggist or pharmacist departs, then force him to open up again for "business."

Some stores allow customers to phone the pharmacist in "emergency" situations, and then meet them at the store for urgently needed prescriptions. Each time a pharmacist responds to this kind of request he is placing his life in danger. One day it won't be the mother who needs something for her child, but a dangerous criminal.

Most pharmacists are aware of the potential hazards. Many store owners, unfortunately, fail to provide the necessary safeguards or safety training for pharmacists or other employees. This can be due to financial considerations or just plain carelessness, but the excuses can never be justified. Safeguards cost very little, especially when they can save large dollar amounts in merchandise or prevent risks to human life. Although law enforcement officials are sometimes blamed when criminals, forced off the streets by police pressure, turn to pharmacies to obtain their drugs, remember that the police must do their jobs and that it's up to businesses to do theirs. Deterring crime through effective security measures and appropriate education and training of employees is an essential business practice.

- Recognize the growing problem of drug abuse and the threat that makes them obvious targets for users and pushers.
- Educate and train employees in precautionary/preventative measures to deter crime.
- Do not respond to telephoned requests for prescriptions by meeting the customer at the store.
- See that every employee receives training in spotting, observing, and reporting suspicious-looking shoppers.
- Make it clear to every employee that he or she should not attempt to interfere with or thwart a robbery at the risk of personal injury or injury to customers.
- Warn employees to be on the lookout for nervous customers who continually walk around and glance towards the pharmacy area. If these persons repeat their visits, especially during opening and closing hours or at shift changes, the new shift of employees should be alerted to their presence and given a brief description of their activities. Employees should attempt to observe their method of transportation and notify the police.
- When in doubt, lock up.
- Limit the amount of narcotics and other dangerous drugs kept on hand. Order only what you need. New supplies are usually readily available.
- Do not arrange drugs in logical, identifiable order; this allows unauthorized individuals to locate them easily.
- Limit access to the pharmacy area to employees.
- Do not allow customers to watch the pharmacist fill prescriptions.
- Do not allow a filled prescription within sight or reach of customers.
- Notify police immediately if a prescription request is fraudulent.
- Maintain adequate staffing.
- Place warning stickers in windows and at counters.
- Make frequent bank deposits.
- Install adequate viewing mirrors, cameras, and one-way glass.
- Install bullet-proof/resistant barriers.

- Keep store windows clear for internal viewing.
- Make sure that pharmacy area can be seen through store windows by police and security patrols.
- Install electronic remote lock switches to control access to the pharmacy area.
- Advertise that only small amounts of drugs are kept on hand.

CHAPTER SIX

Recognizing Threats in the School Environment

One morning Tammy decided that she was "old enough" to walk to the school bus in the morning without Mommy. Mommy, not wanting to treat her daughter like a "baby," agreed.

That same morning, as Tammy proudly joined her friends at the stop, a man drove up in his shiny car and asked her if she would like to go with him and get a jelly donut before school. Before the little girl had a chance to consider the nice man's offer, her bus drove up and she hopped aboard.

Needless to say, the shiny car sped off.

Tammy was lucky. Many others innocently succumb to temptation each year, often to become a sad statistic.

The School Environment

Whether they're in a day care center or on a college campus, students face special threats.

Crime knows no boundaries. It selects the easiest, most vulnerable victim to attack. The ability to recognize a threat is based on the amount of education and training a student receives, most of which begins at home. Whether the recommendations and warnings are heeded is another matter. As a child matures, his or her attitudes concerning crime prevention should mature also. For the teenager attending high school or the college-bound young adult, experience is the best teacher, especially when applied with common sense.

If you're a parent or a young adult looking ahead to graduation, the following suggestions should be useful.

Day Care Centers, Preschool, and Kindergarten

Because children attending preschool or kindergarten classes are usually delivered by parents, relatives, or friends, methods of transportation and their accompanying threats are not discussed here.

It's very important for the parents to fully understand the preschool program they are considering. Most states require preschool and kindergarten facilities and their personnel to meet established legal requirements and standards prior to initiating operation. Study all available material on the school or organization. Ask detailed questions of the staff and of parents and children already attending. Consult your local Board of Education or local government authorities for an in-depth evaluation and recommendation of the school you are considering.

Questions to Ask:

- How long has the center or school been established?
- Is it legally recognized, and is authorization for operation available for review?
- What are the qualifications of the staff? (e.g., education, licenses, etc.)
- Is first aid training a requirement for the staff?
- Is a registered nurse, or a staff member qualified in first aid, available?
- Have there been any accidents, injuries, or deaths within the center? If so, why?
- Do the facilities appear safe?
- Does the facility appear sanitary?
- What form of discipline is administered by the staff?
- If outdoor recreational activities exist, are they safe, and are they supervised 100 percent of the time? Is access available to strangers?

Once you feel satisfied that your children will be cared for by a responsible agency, you should be able to rest a little easier. But it is important to continue your review of the facility, faculty, and other children. Question your children about activities in which they become involved. If it sounds like they are participating in unsafe practices, go and observe a day yourself. If, for any legitimate reason you feel your child's safety and well-being are in jeopardy, pull the child out and report violations to the proper authorities immediately. This may prevent other innocent children from being injured.

What To Tell the Staff:

- All important data pertaining to your child in case of emergency. This includes a list of illnesses, allergies, symptoms, blood type, doctor, hospital, etc. If the staff is directed by you to give your child required medication, they must understand your directions clearly and must be able to recognize danger signals.
- Leave your full name, address and phone number where you can be reached if you're not at home, and a back-up number of a friend or relative who can assist during an emergency.
- Never allow anyone except designated parents or relatives pick your child up from the center. If this rule is broken, even once, pull your children out of the center. One mistake is all that it takes.
- If friends and neighbors are driving the children on a rotating or carpooling basis, make sure they have permission, in writing, to pick up the children. Identify exactly whom they may take.

It is always a good idea to call the center in advance (same day) to tell them who is picking up your child. If staff is in any doubt, they should call the parents for release approval, or, as a last resort, keep the child at the center until you can come to get him. This may cause a little trouble and time delay, but not when compared with having a stranger kidnap your child. This requirement should allow you to sleep better! If children are regularly picked up by someone other than their parents, this person should be photographed and the photograph kept on file for immediate identification.

Along with the normal counseling that parents provide their children, they should tell them to:

- Inform their parents of any problems, or strange or dangerous activities that they become involved with or exposed to.
- Report all strangers that approach them.
- Never leave the center or school with any stranger.
- Never engage in any activity that frightens them or is wrong.

Grades 1-12

The following additional concerns are important for older students:

- How does the student get to and from school?
- What activities does the student engage in before and after school?
- What freedoms are allowed the student (e.g., driving, dating)? Are they safe? Are they appropriate for his age level?
- Is the parent aware of the student's location and times of return?

Student Safety Tips

- Never leave school without your parent's knowledge.
- Never leave school with a stranger.
- Never hitchhike to or from school.
- Lock all lockers (hall and gym). Never give out your combination to friends, or leave the combination on the last number so that it requires only a spin to open it.
- Never take large sums of money or valuables to school.
- Report all crime to the school's main office.
- If you or other students are experiencing emotional difficulties linked to domestic problems or drug and alcohol abuse, or have any other problem, request the assistance of counselors for support and advice.

College

Many college-bound students will spend the next four or more years away from home. Good security habits should be developed to protect both your valuables and your life during this period. Plan to combine the home environment procedures discussed earlier with the following additional recommendations:

Room/Dorm Security Questions to Consider:

- Does your room and facility have adequate door and window locks and lighting?
- Do you share your room or facility with another student?
- Does your roommate practice crime prevention?
- Do you have a complete inventory of all your valuables?
- Who else has keys to your room and facility?
- Will the college rekey your room or facility door if requested? Will they allow you to obtain and pay for this service? (It's worth it, even if you have to pay for it yourself.)
- Does your room have a telephone?
- Do you know the local police/security, fire, and rescue telephone numbers? Are they posted on or near your telephone, along with your complete address?
- Is there an emergency fire exit plan in your facility? Do you know where the emergency fire exits are?

Campus Tips

- Make sure that the college student center/administration office maintains your emergency/next of kin information.
- Never travel alone, especially at night.
- Never take shortcuts across campus that are unfamiliar or unsafe.
- Never hitchhike.
- Never run, jog or exercise outside at night alone.
- Always lock your vehicle or bicycle up properly.
- Never allow your room to be left unlocked or leave visitors in your room alone, unescorted.
- Never allow strangers to enter your room.
- Never give your room key to another person.

Check your college security department for additional advice on crime prevention and security.

Threats to Teachers

Crime within the school is reported to be on the increase, particularly in large inner-city schools. Obviously the more crime experienced in a school, the greater the likelihood that a teacher will be assaulted.

Teachers are under heavy job pressures. More than 80 percent of new teachers that leave their chosen profession do so within a one- to two-year period, often because they fail to establish and maintain discipline within their classrooms. Many feel forced out of teaching and become disenchanted with their original dreams of educating young people. In some cases, teachers do not receive the support they need from their administration for disciplinary actions taken on students. Consequently, teachers are vulnerable to the criticism and scorn of angry parents.

Blackboard jungles do exist, and for many teachers it can be a day-to-day fight for survival. The increase in crime in the schools coupled with the freedoms experienced by young people today, make establishing and maintaining control and discipline extremely difficult. Both verbal and physical confrontation are increasing, and they often end with the assault of a teacher in the classroom, the hallway, or the parking lot. If the teacher is not personally attacked, their residence may be vandalized or their family harassed.

In most cases, teachers are able to control their students and maintain adequate discipline. The individual personalities and capabilities of teachers are the major factors in creating a classroom environment that is conducive to learning. No written guidelines can prepare a teacher for every possible crisis. Communication is probably the single most necessary element in a successful teacher/pupil relationship. When communication breaks down, the opportunity for confrontation increases.

Verbal confrontations challenge many teachers on a daily basis. Whether it's dismissal from the class or suspension from school, the possibility of physical violence is real. Some students will attempt to intimidate a teacher, using the support of a few close classmates. If the teacher loses his or her cool and becomes visibly shaken, the student is likely to continue until the teacher either turns away admitting loss of control, or out of frustration begins a verbal debate. This kind of situation often ends in a shouting match, and may turn into a violent physical struggle. A teacher should in all cases attempt to avoid an all-out fight. But when faced with a student attempting assault, the teacher should defend against injury while employing passive restraining techniques as described in Chapter 15. When a teacher feels that he or she may become a target of an angry student, the following precautions should be taken:

- Report possible threats to school administrators and to the police.
- Remain in the company of other teachers.
- Park vehicles in a visible location for protection against vandalism.
- Advise your family to be aware of any strange or unusual activity.
- Increase home protection with lights, locks, etc.
- Avoid secluded areas such as locker rooms and restrooms before, during, and after school activities.

Based on the experiences of teachers who have been faced with disciplinary problems, the following list of recommendations has been developed to help avoid confrontations in the classroom.

- Establish effective communication with students, and get the support of school administration.
- Involve all students in establishing rules for the classroom, but be sure they understand who is the teacher and who is the student. Help students understand that no organization can survive without order and discipline, and explain how nobody wins when there is anarchy.
- Establish a bond of trust, fairness, and respect with your students.
- Make sure the students understand your directions clearly.
- Avoid sarcasm, shouting matches, and embarrassing or chastising a student in front of classmates. You may create a confrontation by backing him into a corner.
- Never threaten punishment unless you are willing to carry it out.
- Identify problem students and determine how to handle them. Recommend counseling when it is obvious that a student is suffering from domestic or drug and alcohol problems. Try to become more than just a teacher, but a

friend who is concerned. Students respect this. Identify the dangerous students and take whatever steps are necessary to insure a safe environment for other students and teachers.

- Walk a mile in the student's shoes. Try to experience their accomplishments as well as their pressures and failures.
- Recognize accomplishments of students and provide positive reinforcement when possible.
- Never underestimate the power a teacher has. Most students look up to teachers and heed their comments. A single recommendation can build—or destroy—a career.

CHAPTER SEVEN

Recognizing Threats in the Recreational Environment

Hard-luck Jack had only carried luggage at the sumptuous Oceanview Inn for three months. His minimum wages, nickel-dime tips and the long, hard hours, increased his resentment of the guests who could afford the luxuries he only dreamed of.

With easy access to the room keys, Jack decided one day to get lucky and then get out of town.

Stashing jewelry, cash, cameras, and clothing into a suitcase, he was long-gone before anything was missed. Not an hour away, Jack was already plotting his next rip-off—"It was so easy to lift the goodies all those trusting tourists left behind," he mused. "It'll be even easier next time!"

Perhaps the most vulnerable time of our lives is during that period of extreme mental and physical relaxation commonly known as the vacation. This is a time to forget our troubles, not to add more to our list!

Depending on how much time and money people have available, their vacation may range from a one-day shopping spree to a months-long cross-country excursion. But just because we relax and try to forget the daily hustle and bustle we left behind, doesn't mean that the criminal element is also relaxing. Indeed, professional and amateur criminals alike eagerly await the vacationing tourist who is temporarily hypnotized by the sights and sounds of the vacation area. Never—especially at vacation time—relax your awareness to your immediate environment. (If you're not yet thinking "awareness," you should be by the time you finish this book.)

So unless you intend to spend your hard-earned vacation boarded up in the sanctuary of your home, be prepared to expect the unexpected.

Effective Planning

Planning for your vacation should include a careful, well-organized checklist of priorities. Too often, an excited family forgets a small essential task or leaves behind a simple object, only to suffer later for the oversight. By taking the time to arrange priorities in a logical, common-sense format, a schedule can be designed to cover the necessary items and lay the groundwork for a safe and enjoyable vacation.

Begin by gathering the family together for a discussion so that everyone can contribute to the vacation checklist. Be sure to cover the entire vacation from beginning to end. By involving each family member you indirectly place responsibility on everyone's shoulders. This makes everyone feel needed, and helps to develop a responsible attitude as well.

While the family is together, cover the basic principles of family safety and security. Inform everyone of the potential hazards and dangers that exist and what to do if exposed to them. Encourage questions and quiz your children about simple situations that they may run into. To simply say "Stick close," or "Don't talk to strangers," is not enough, even though this is just about all that many families cover during a family outing. By discussing what could happen, you are likely to prompt questions that will educate your family and prevent involvement in a dangerous situation. The answers should come from you before involvement, not afterwards, based on experience that may place a family member in danger. By making each person aware of what can happen, they will begin to question whether involvement in a certain activity is safe. "What could happen if . . . ?," or, "How will this effect me or my family?" Once they start thinking this way, their own individual awareness of potential dangers will increase.

Precautions to Take When Leaving for Vacation

Many homes are broken into and vandalized because the owners made it very clear that nobody would be home to stop them. A home that looks occupied stands a better chance of escaping burglary than one that appears deserted.

When you are planning a long vacation, or just an evening out, you must always secure your home. Before you depart on your vacation, always:

- Inform the police of your absence and ask them, when possible, to patrol the area and keep an eye out for any suspicious activity.
- Leave a key to your home with trusted neighbors, and ask them to inform the police of any suspicious activity.
- Leave several lights on throughout your home. If you are to be gone for a long period of time, use a timer switch device which activates the lights, the radio, and the television at different intervals to leave the impression that the house is occupied. Make sure that all timer devices are safe, or as an alternative, ask your neighbor to turn on these appliances for you.
- Leave blinds or shades in their normal positions.
- Always arrange to have your lawn mowed and any snow plowed or shoveled from your driveway. Stop all newspaper, mail and dairy deliveries, or arrange to have them picked up regularly.
- Take all your valuables to a safe deposit box, or leave them with a trusted relative or friend.
- Do not discuss your vacation plans or schedules with anyone except your trusted neighbor or close relative.
- Never leave notes on your door telling when you will return.
- Arrange to have garbage cans used by a neighbor, who will set out any garbage for pick-up.
- If you own two vehicles and take only one on vacation, park the remaining one in the space where the primary vehicle is normally parked.
- Turn the ringer volume down on your telephone.
- Ask your neighbor to make several security checks of your residence while you are gone. You can return the favor when your neighbor leaves for his vacation.

Family Identification

Each member of your family, including the baby, should carry some form of identification. Why are we so careful to tag our luggage with our identification, yet neglect to properly identify our family members? Many parents would respond, "My child doesn't need any identification because he never leaves my side." But what if one day that child gets separated from his mother and father?

FAMILY IDENTIFICATION

Front

Name:_____ Age:_____

Home Address: _____ **PHOTO**

Home Phone Number: (_____)_____

Parents Names Are:_____

Next of Kin: _____ Phone:_____

Special Medications: _____

_____ Blood Type:_____

Allergies/Reactions:_____

Misc. Data: _____

Rear

Daily Itinerary

Temp. Address: (ie., Hotel/Motel-Room number) _____

Phone Number: (_____)_____

Vehicle ID: Make:_____ Model:_____

Year:_____ Color:_____ License Number:_____

Currently Parked At: _____

Estimated Time of Departure: _____

Family Is Currently At: _____

Figure 7-1

Every person, no matter how old, should carry an identification card (Figure 7-1). The card should include normal identification information as well as special data such as blood type, allergies, required medication, and information about conditions such as heart trouble or high blood pressure. An identification card can be made for each child at home and encased in plastic. This card can be carried in a variety of ways, including being attached to a necklace or pinned to a piece of clothing.

Another good idea is for each vacationing family member to carry a daily itinerary. It would contain temporary data, such as where the family is staying, and vehicle identification, including its current location and what time all are expected to return to the vehicle. This itinerary may be stuffed in a pocket or taped to the back of the member's identification card. Now if "little Johnny" is accidentally separated from Mom and Dad at the amusement park, the good Samaritan or security officer who finds him will have comprehensive information to work with. Not only do they know who "Johnny" is, they also know he is there with his family, temporarily staying at a certain hotel, and that their vehicle is currently parked outside the amusement park in Row F. Helpful? You bet!

Along with providing their identification cards, you must tell your children that if they are separated from you there are certain people who will help them find you. Tell them to look for a policeman or a person dressed up like one (security guard), while pointing one out to them. If one is not available, then they should approach a concession stand and ask for help. Under no circumstances are they to exit the park *without* Mommy or Daddy!

Special Items

Always double-check before departing to be sure that you have those special items that cannot be easily replaced, such as medicines, an extra pair of glasses or contact lenses, credit cards, etc.

Inventory of Valuables

Before you leave, prepare a complete inventory of valuables you are taking with you (camera, radio, etc.) in case they are stolen while on vacation. Be sure to include any identification numbers or codes. Leave one copy with a neighbor or friend, and take another with you.

Public Transportation

If you and your family are planning to travel by public transportation, take the following precautionary measures to help avoid problems:

- Understand all travel plans and transportation transfers completely.
- Lock all luggage and mark it with complete identification, including home address and phone number. Tags can be torn off, so it's best to mark directly on the surface of the luggage.
- Never leave baggage tags on from previous trips. These might lead to a misrouting of your luggage.
- Never travel with contraband or dangerous items.
- Carry all currency and credit cards with you. (Preferably leave what you don't need at home.)
- Carry travelers checks instead of large sums of cash.
- Obtain insurance on high-value items prior to travel.
- Never leave carry-on luggage (e.g., briefcase, purse) unattended.
- Never leave children unattended.
- Understand each form of public transportation you plan to use. Transferring from one bus, train, or plane to another can be a frustrating experience. Plan ahead, and don't be afraid or embarrassed to ask for help.

If you are traveling by train, always secure your belongings prior to leaving your individual compartment. When traveling, especially in crowded situations, keep an eye out for pickpockets, particularly the stranger next to you.

Accommodations

When taking a vacation also means staying in a hotel or motel, there are several important items to consider. Remember, the area you've chosen is probably new and unfamiliar, so stay where you feel most comfortable.

Tips for a Safer Stay

- Always try to locate a well-kept hotel or motel in a highly visible, well-lighted area. Avoid back-street locations that can conceal criminals.

- When you check into your lodgings, study all procedures and attitudes towards guests. Poor service in the lobby is a possible indicator of poor room conditions.

- If you are staying in a motel, park directly in front of your assigned room if possible. If poor parking accommodations require you to isolate your vehicle at any great distance, look for another establishment. As a last resort, park in front of the motel office.

- When you have been assigned a room, test the door lock and survey the room closely for security or safety hazards.

- Once inside, close the blinds before unpacking your luggage. There is no need to advertise what you have with you.

- When unloading your vehicle, never leave your room or vehicle unattended if unlocked. If you are alone, take the time to lock the car trunk or door before leaving for your room. Trunks left open while you step inside your room may offer passersby a view of your luggage, as well as a possible free gift.

- Lock anything left in your vehicle inside the trunk. Any highly valuable items should always be locked up in the hotel/motel safe, and be sure to get a receipt. **NOTE:** There are probably many keys that will open your room door. Your room can be opened with the hotel master key by maids, maintenance men, etc. Most hotels warn that you leave items in your room at your own risk, so don't ask for trouble by leaving your camera or watch inside the room when you go out. Many hotel and motel keys are lost or stolen, and the locks they fit are never changed. This creates not only a property risk problem, but a personal risk as well.

- Always use the door lock and security chain when inside your room.

- Be sure to lock your door and double check it anytime you return to your room. It's also a good idea to place a room chair behind your door to hinder any unexpected entrances. This will not, of course, prevent a person from making a forceful entrance, but it will usually provide enough racket to warn you.

- Never leave children alone in your room or in the lobby.
- If a maintenance man is required, always contact the hotel desk and confirm the worker upon arrival at the door of your room.
- Never leave valuables lying around. Always lock them in your vehicle when going out.
- Never flash money around in public.
- Never inform strangers of your employment position or how long you intend to be away.
- Never go to the pool and leave your room key lying next to you with your towel.
- Never leave children alone at the pool.
- Never leave children alone in the restroom or the shower room. Accompany them or wait outside for them.
- When leaving your room, expect maid service, so be sure to secure your property accordingly.
- Never walk to your room in the dark. Stay in the light and ask for an escort if you are concerned.
- Leave a light on if you intend to return at night. Upon returning to your room, peak inside the window, if possible, to insure your room is empty. If the light is off, don't panic. Possibly the maid was in earlier and turned it off; however, don't take any chances. It could mean someone is waiting inside for you. Always enter with caution. By all means never enter a room when you think someone could be waiting inside.

When parked at a hotel/motel out-of-state, consider how obvious it is to the surrounding community. Your vehicle license plate identifies you as a stranger passing through, making you a prime target for the local criminal who realizes that you probably are only in town for a night or two. The criminal also knows that you probably will not stick around long enough to be concerned with a missing camera or other relatively small item, and that in most cases you probably won't even report the theft to the local police.

If your room or vehicle is broken into, notify the local police immediately. Provide the police with a complete description of items stolen (from the inventory list you prepared prior to departure). You probably will never see your property again, but if, by chance, it is recovered, the police should notify you. Always get a complete copy of the police report/investigation to keep for future use, as well as for insurance purposes.

When You Check Out

- Make sure to thoroughly search your room for items you may have forgotten.
- Obtain valuables secured in the hotel safe.
- Pay your bill, return your key, and leave the souvenir towel or ash tray in the room where it belongs.

Activities

When involved in activities like sightseeing or visiting the zoo or amusement park, be sure everyone has an identification card. Make sure everyone understands the planned activities and knows what to do if separated. A time schedule should be set up and adhered to. Each person should be able to remember what the others are wearing (identify colors, etc.), so that they can locate one another if separated. Always inform each other of unscheduled activities, and never split up without both taking someone along and informing the other family members where you plan to be. Inform each other when entering a restroom, and leave your purse or souvenirs with another family member waiting outside for your return. Make sure to carry only the money you need, and never place it in just one pocket. Place your credit cards and cash in separate front pockets, remaining alert for pickpockets and purse snatchers. All purses, cameras, etc., should be securely held and never left unattended. It is also a good idea to locate a police or security officer and identify him to your children so they are able to recognize him, if needed.

Coming Home

1. If you find a door or window open, do not enter. Use your neighbor's phone and call the police immediately. The criminal may still be inside.
2. Conduct a complete inspection of your home and all property.
3. If you arrive home by taxi, ask the driver to accompany you to your door.
4. Always have your keys in hand for extra protection as you open the door.

5. Keep a sharp watch out for strangers or strange vehicles nearby. If you notice any unusual disturbance or have any uneasy feelings, call the police.
6. Let your neighbor know you're home (especially if returning in the middle of the night) or slide a note under his door.
7. Now unpack your luggage, put on your robe and slippers, click your heels together three times, and repeat, "There's no place like home..."

CHAPTER EIGHT

Consumer Fraud: Beware the Wolf in Sheep's Clothing

A 70-year-old grandmother was called on by a salesman trying to sell her an insurance policy that offered unlimited reimbursement for medical bills, at a cost of only $10.00 per month. The only thing Grandma had to do was give the salesman $2,500 up front in order for the policy to take effect. Wise Grandma excused herself to "turn off the stove." Instead she made a quick phone call to the insurance company only to discover that her "salesman" was wanted for stealing blank policy certificates. She then made another call to the police. While she poured the salesman his second cup of tea, police arrived and took him away.

Beware the Wolf in Sheep's Clothing
Each year thousands of unsuspecting families become victims of fraud. Con artists thrive on schemes, scams, rip-offs, and swindles, walking away from trusting individuals with millions of their hard-earned dollars. Most of the victims who feel the sting of these scams find it too embarrassing to admit that they were fooled, and often fail to report the crime to their local police.

What we are talking about here is the deliberate act of intent to mislead a potential customer into purchasing a product that is usually of poor quality, or forcing the signing of a contract under high-pressure sales tactics. This is not to say that legitimate sales people do not exist—of course they do. Many professionals and ethical business people are involved in door-to-door, telephone, and mail advertising campaigns. What you need to watch out for are the hundreds of unethical, crooked, flim-flam artists who claim to represent legitimate businesses offering quality products and honorable guarantees. Unfortunately, these criminals give the honest, hardworking salesperson a bad name. Like the old saying, "One bad apple can spoil the bunch." The consumer must learn to distinguish between the "bad apples" and the rest of the "bunch."

Who is the Victim?

Anyone can unknowingly fall prey to a con artist, but in some cases specific targets are preyed on because of their inexperience and obvious weaknesses.

The senior citizen is a prime example. Most seniors are very friendly and trusting and enjoy the company of anyone who shows an interest in conversation with them. Elderly people often lead lonely lives and are hungry for companionship. And since the fear of crime on the street forces many to remain in the confines of their home or retirement center, they find it convenient to buy products from door-to-door sales people or through the mail. Most are looking for a reliable product that they can afford on their fixed incomes. Unfortunately, errors in judgment can result from such handicaps as sight or hearing loss, and they are often easy to take advantage of because of infirmities or emotional conditions. They are frequently the targets of high-pressure tactics and pushed or forced to sign on the dotted line.

Another group heavily favored to be victimized are young people. Their lack of experience with high pressure sales tactics and naivete can make them easy marks for the experienced con, even though they try to act responsibly. Too many gain their experience the hard way, after losing their money to a swindler.

Then there are the rest of us—the housewife who gets taken advantage of by a service station mechanic, or the businessman who gets ripped off by a plumber, electrician, or office-supply dealer.

Methods of Fraud

Door-to-Door Salespersons

- Beware of the so-called "free gift." It's usually a gimmick to get you to buy something expensive.
- Any time you purchase an item from a door-to-door salesperson that costs $25 or more, you are supposed to

receive a written contract, along with at least two Notice of Cancellation forms. If you should change your mind, you have up to three days to cancel your order. (Check with your state laws.)

- Anyone selling a product door-to-door should be checked out through the Better Business Bureau or Consumer Affairs Office.
- Never purchase medical supplies, insurance, or equipment without first checking out the company. Never purchase "medicines" from salespersons.
- Never buy land without seeing it first.
- Never sign a work contract for home repairs without checking the business out through the Better Business Bureau or Consumer Affairs Office.
- Beware the person who says one thing outside your home, but once inside, quickly or schemingly changes his motives for being there. Someone who will lie or trick you to gain entrance will also stoop to trickery to gain a sale.

  This person may also be posing as a representative for a survey or opinion poll, while actually casing or studying your home for his next robbery.
- Never buy a product because the salesperson uses scare tactics like "It's for your own good." Never be pressured into any sale.
- Never sign a contract without reading it and understanding it fully. It is always wise to seek legal advice on any contract.
- If the salesperson avoids your questions or does not have the answers, do not purchase the product.

Mail Order Scams

- Always understand what you are buying and how much it is going to cost you.
- Never send cash through the mail.
- Federal law requires most mail order firms to fill your order within thirty days unless stated otherwise. If you fail to receive your order within the thirty days, you may cancel, and the company must refund your money within seven days.
- Be concerned about the "free gift" offers or the grand prize you have just won, especially if you did not enter the contest. Most of these techniques are used to lure you into

buying products you never wanted or never intended to purchase.

- If you receive something by mail that you did not order, don't open it. Mark it "Return to Sender" and mail it back.

- "Earn a degree at home." Many advertised home study or improvement courses promise an "accredited degree" (but accredited by whom?), with the possibility of helping you locate a job after successfully completing the course. These programs usually request a fairly large enrollment fee (non-refundable) and offer no guarantees. Legitimate home study and college-level degree programs do operate by mail, but read the fine print to be sure.

Home Improvement/Repair

Watch out for the person who attempts to convince you that you need home repairs that they can perform at a special rate. Common examples: resurfacing your driveway with a cheap resurfacing material, fixing your roof, or building an addition onto your home. These people usually require an advance, if not payment-in-full, prior to work, then skip out of town leaving the work half completed, if started at all. If the work is completed, it is usually with inferior materials, which last just long enough for them to get away. Any guarantees offered should be closely examined and their business credentials confirmed before you sign any contract. Again, contact the local Better Business Bureau or Consumer Affairs Office.

Health Insurance

The cost of medical services has risen dramatically. For many, especially senior citizens receiving Medicare, the necessary treatment is unaffordable. But all one has to do is read magazine articles and watch television to realize that there are many different insurance programs available that will cover expenses that their current medical insurance and/or Medicare will not. Legitimate? Maybe, but too many are designed for only one reason: to take advantage of those in need and desperate for help. There are good insurance programs advertised, but are they exactly what you need? Take the proper time to investigate them. Write your state Insurance Commissioner or Better Business Bureau. Above all, before you purchase an insurance policy, be sure it contains what it is supposed to cover, and make sure you understand it completely.

Con Games

Bait-and-Switch Routine: Some businesses offer or advertise a particular product for a certain price. When you try to purchase this product you are told, "We're all sold out," or, "It's really not what you need." Then the salesperson attempts to sell you another similar product for more money, usually playing on your pride and conscience to, "Spend a little more for the added protection or performance. Your family is worth it."

Earn Money at Home: Many ads offer "large sums of money in a few short weeks for working in the privacy of your own home!" Most only want your money, in advance, and then supply you with worthless advice or impractical and expensive "get rich quick" schemes.

The Pigeon Drop: This is a very old and effective con game that has stolen more money from the unwary than most others combined. First, a stranger begins a conversation with you. He or she will always be neatly dressed, and will be very polite and courteous. Pretty soon they tell you that they have stumbled onto a very large sum of money, and eventually will offer you a share. "There is enough for the both of us." Once you agree to help, or indicate you would like to make some easy money, you will be asked to put up some "good faith" money before you can receive your part of the cash. Once you provide your good faith money, you'll never see it or the swindler again.

The Obituary Column Trick: A con man will read of the recent death of a spouse or relative in the paper. He will then arrive in person or send a request in the mail referring to a debt that was left unpaid by the recently departed, and request payment. Usually, the victim is still in mourning and pays the bill before it is completely checked out. Any legitimate person or organization should understand the delay in payment in a case such as this. Also, beware the person who arrives with a very expensive bible or other related object, possibly with an engraving or inscription on it from the deceased, with instructions that it was to be delivered to the surviving spouse upon death, *cash on delivery*. Surely, if your loved one had taken the necessary time to order a gift for an occasion such as this, it would have been paid for in advance. Request an order invoice, or receipt, with a valid signature on it to confirm the sale, or forget it.

Consumer Rights

The following is a look at common everyday concerns that effect everyone across the country. These consumer rights apply to most U.S. states, but you should research exactly what rights exist in your area. This can be done by contacting your local Consumer Affairs Office.

Auto Repair

All dealers or service stations providing repairs must:

- Give you a written estimate if the cost is over $25 unless you turn it down in writing. The final charges may not be more than 10 percent over the original estimate unless you authorized such repair and additional costs. (Providers of certain professional services, such as lawyers, doctors, and dentists, are not required to provide estimates.)
- Provide you with a copy of any document you have signed.
- Provide you a complete list of all itemized items, their costs, including labor, and cannot charge you for things not listed or related to repairs unless you were notified in advance, and cannot claim a repair that is or was not needed.
- Provide you with all replaced parts unless you were told in advance that they would not be returned, or indicated you did not want them.

Telephone Requests for Repairs or Service

When you request information pertaining to repairs or service over the phone, you are authorized to receive estimates orally, and then to receive a written one before any work is performed. In addition, when calling for towing service, you must be informed of the service charge, cost per mile, and any other related charge for service.

Refunds

Every person is entitled to a full refund for any item purchased by cash or check when it is returned in its original condition, unless a sign was posted conspicuously that stated you must have a receipt, or if the sign stated a "NO REFUND" policy.

Deposits

Any time you place a deposit on an item, you are entitled to a dated receipt and information that specifically states the time limit it will be held for you, the total cost, and whether the deposit is refundable or not.

Beware of:

- High pressure sales tactics.
- "Buy now, or forget it," or "Buy now, because tomorrow the price will go up."
- "Act now, and get your free gift."
- "Earn high wages quickly and easily in the comfort and privacy of your own home."
- "You have been selected as one of our winners..."
- "Cash only," and usually in advance.
- Sales that offer no guarantees.

Never:

- Sign a contract until you have reviewed it thoroughly or have had it reviewed for you.
- Agree to withdraw money from your bank account based on a request from a so-called bank representative to help "catch a dishonest employee."
- Engage in any scheme that offers "quick and easy cash." They rarely exist. Verify all transactions through at least two reputable sources.
- Allow anyone into your home without proper identification, especially those individuals who appear strange or under the influence of alcohol or drugs. When in doubt, leave them out. You don't have to let anyone in your home if you don't want to. It's your home.
- Open any mail not addressed to you or that you did not order. Mark "Return to Sender" and let the postal service return it with no charge to you.

Always:

- Get a signed, dated receipt for any item you purchase.
- Keep all paperwork related to a purchase.
- When in doubt, contact the sales company supplying the product to confirm a sales representative or to have your questions answered and any complaints taken care of.
- When considering purchasing a product, stop and think if you really need it, and if it is reliable.
- Be sure all family members and house employees are aware of fraud and are familiar with how to handle it.
- Get a written estimate when requesting any repairs and services.
- Learn to say NO!

- Report any suspicious activity or individual(s) to the police immediately.
- Contact your local Better Business Bureau or Consumer Affairs Office when in doubt about any sales activity as well as to confirm the reliability and performance of a product.
- Determine if a sales company is local. Obtain a complete address and phone number and confirm it if you feel concerned.
- Report a fraud to your local police, the Better Business Bureau, and Consumer Affairs Office. Put an end to it now to keep it from claiming another victim.
- Consider taking fraudulent persons and businesses to Small Claims Court.

Remember, very rarely will you get something for nothing. Somewhere you will pay the price. Learn to fight back by being on the lookout for fraud. Slam the door in its face and send the con artist away with the knowledge that the consumer is becoming harder to swindle.

For More Information, Contact:

- Federal Trade Commission: for information pertaining to false or deceptive sales activities, when the manufacturer of the product is located out of state.
- U.S. Postal Service: for information and advice pertaining to mail fraud or violations.
- Better Business Bureau
- Consumer Affairs Office
- State Attorney General's Office
- U.S. Consumer Product Safety Commission
- State Public Utility Commission: for utility problems.
- Local police.
- County Prosecutor's Office.

CHAPTER NINE

Protecting Your Transportation

Ed, excited over his brand new motorcycle, stopped outside of his friend Jill's apartment to show it off. In his haste, he forgot to remove the ignition key. Racing back with Jill, both watched in disbelief as the new motorcycle disappeared over the hill, ridden by a "new" owner.

Motor Vehicle Theft

More than a million vehicles are stolen in the United States each year. That's one out of every 150 registered in this country. Of these thefts, about 800,000 were actually "gifts," because they were left unlocked with their windows rolled down, and about 200,000 of them had keys left in the ignition. Based on these figures, one out of five vehicles is never recovered. According to the FBI Crime Index, a vehicle is stolen every 29 seconds, two-thirds of them at night. Over 50 percent occur in residential neighborhoods. These figures do not include the millions of vehicles that have parts stolen or are vandalized, which constitute 37 percent of the nation's auto crimes. On the average 75 percent of the stolen vehicles reported are autos, 14 percent are trucks and buses. The remaining 11 percent are other types of motor vehicles.

The average motor vehicle thief is twenty-one years old or younger. Most vehicles are stolen by amateurs looking for quick money or a joy ride, and because the opportunity was there—the keys were frequently left in the ignition.

There's a lot you can do to keep the amateur from stealing your vehicle, but if the professional wants it, he will usually get it. The best you can do is to practice good security habits, and maintain appropriate insurance coverage in case of loss. Above all, keep complete, accurate, and up-to-date records on all vehicles. At a minimum, maintain the following:

- Vehicle identification number
- Hull identification number (on boats)
- Year, make, and model
- Engine size
- Color
- License number and state (for both vehicle and trailer, if applicable)
- Any unusual details or markings

If your vehicle is stolen, report it to the police immediately with this identification information.

When Purchasing a Vehicle

When you decide to buy a new or used vehicle, always be sure you are not getting one that is "hot," or stolen. Always buy from a reputable dealer. Private sales are fine, but beware of the smooth, "too good to be true" deals. If you are suspicious, contact the police.

If you buy your car from a private individual, make sure that the person you deal with has a listed address and phone number and is not a traveling salesman. Check all paperwork and be sure listed serial/vehicle identification numbers match, and that they have not been tampered with or changed. Also be sure the license plates are valid. If in doubt, check with the local police. Do all the keys fit, and do they work properly? Always request a receipt at the time of purchase, along with a witnessed bill of sale that includes all the necessary data (social security number, identification number, odometer reading).

Following is a list of tips to help deter the theft of your vehicle. The easiest and usually most effective technique is to simply lock all doors, roll up the windows, and remove the ignition key! In addition, always:

- Park in a visible location, away from alleys, abandoned buildings, etc.

- If you have a garage, use it and keep it locked.
- Park in a well-lighted area.
- Use a vehicle alarm system if possible.
- Advertise with a sticker that your vehicle has an alarm system.
- Lock all valuables (CB, tape deck, shopping bags) in the trunk.
- Use an anti-theft lock or device to lock the steering column when possible.
- When parked at a curb, always angle the front tires into the curb at approximately a 45 degree angle, preventing easy towing by thieves.
- Do not leave a vehicle abandoned or parked in any location (away from home) for long periods of time.
- Apply ignition "cut-off" devices, or pull the coil wire from the distributor when leaving a vehicle at an unknown location for several hours.
- Never leave the vehicle title or registration inside your vehicle.
- Place special markings on your vehicle to assist in identification if stolen and then recovered. Drop a business or identification card down inside the door for future identification.
- When parking in a commercial lot, never give the attendant all your keys, just the ignition/door key; always remove any valuables. Most lots warn that they are not responsible for lost or missing items. Try to avoid this type of parking lot if possible.
- Check license plates, especially if from out of town, to insure that they have not been stolen or switched.

Motorcycles and Bicycles

A large number of bikes are stolen each year for the same reasons that cars and trucks are. Too many are left unattended and unlocked, which make them easy targets for the thief. If you want your property secure, you have to take proper measures to keep it secure.

To start with, record the serial number/identification number of your bike and keep it stored with other valuable papers, so that you can, when appropriate, provide the police with a complete description. Many police departments have bicycle registration programs set up for this purpose. Take a color photo and keep it with the other identification data.

In addition to the existing serial number, or if no identification number exists, you might want to engrave your social security number or other important number on your bike to help identify it.

Always carry a lock and chain that will secure your bike effectively. Make sure the lock is practical and efficient and the chain is strong enough to withstand a good deal of punishment. When using a chain or cable, always secure the front and back wheels to a solid, permanent fixture. On most motorcycles, there is a front fork lock built in, or a place for a padlock, that should be utilized every time you leave your bike. Treat your bike with respect and never leave it lying around. You can also park your bike between a wall and your car. This will slow down a thief. If you don't take care of it, you might lose it. There are many people who would like to have your bike who, unfortunately, might take it off your hands permanently.

Boat Theft

Boat theft is on the increase, and is fast becoming a very lucrative illegal business. Thousands of private and commercial vessels are stolen each year. In 1982 alone, over 23,761 boats were reported stolen, according to *FBI Magazine*. When entire boats cannot be successfully obtained, their engines, instruments, and other expensive parts are removed. It is estimated that over $60 million is lost annually in the theft of boats and related marine equipment.

Certain measures can and must be taken to help deter, and in some cases eliminate, the chance of theft. All boats are required by state and federal law to have individual titles and registrations. These requirements simplify the tracing of stolen vessels and increase the likelihood of return to the rightful owner.

Titling and registration is currently required in 45 of the 50 United States. Unfortunately, uniform guidelines have not yet been established between states to provide effective boat titling procedures and records systems that would help states determine valid ownership of stolen boats.

The 1971 Federal Boat Safety Act mandated that all boats manufactured for sale within the United States be marked by the manufacturer with a twelve-character "Hull Identification

Number" (HIN). This number is used to help the manufacturer maintain quality control of inventory, and also to protect the buyer in ways that allow proper identification of model year. Boat manufacturers were not required to give their products an HIN prior to 1971. HINs are a great aid in locating a stolen boat.

Identification and serial numbers are extremely important in verifying ownership, but might not always be necessary if owners would take proper measures to secure their property. Consider how simple it can be for a person to back his vehicle up to a boat mounted on a trailer, hook it up, and drive away. This happens in broad daylight, not just in the dead of night. The same is true for boats left unlocked and unattended, floating in the water, when it is even simpler for a thief since all he has to do is start it up and speed away to a waiting trailer. By practicing good boat safety and security, you can enjoy your free time in the water, instead of being left high and dry ashore.

Anti-Theft Tips for Boats

- Understand your state and local laws pertaining to boat ownership/operation.
- Understand existing systems to help prevent theft of boats and equipment.
- Know how to report stolen equipment, and to whom.
- Keep up-to-date photos of your boat and equipment.
- Maintain a complete inventory of equipment and a detailed listing of serial numbers, hull identification numbers, etc. Affix your own private identification marks in secret locations.
- Maintain adequate insurance coverage.
- Lock at least two parts of the trailer to a permanent fixture.
- Chain the engine securely, or remove it and lock it inside a building or the cabin of the boat.
- If your boat is mounted on a trailer parked in your yard or driveway, make sure that it cannot be towed away by unauthorized means.
- Never leave your boat ignition key with the boat.
- Remove a wheel from the trailer if it is to be parked for a long period of time.
- Remove the battery.

- Never leave a "for sale" sign in a parked boat. People will assume the thief is looking to buy.
- Report any suspicious activity or individuals around your boat or the marina to the police immediately.

When your boat is stolen, notify:

- Local and State Police who will in turn contact the National Crime Information Center (NCIC) and the FBI.
- U.S. Coast Guard, who will also notify NCIC and the FBI.
- Marina or storage manager and dealer from whom boat was purchased, who will in turn notify the Marine Trade Association (hot lists) and boat manufacturer.
- Insurance company, who will notify the National Theft Reporting and Recovery Bureaus.
- Neighbors and nearby marina.

Aircraft Theft

Stealing aircraft usually requires a bit more sophistication than stealing land or water vehicles, but it is steadily increasing in popularity among criminals. An estimated $25 million in aircraft was stolen in 1981. The big advantage in aircraft theft is that the thief is not restricted by roads or water. All that is necessary to "fly" away with a plane is knowledge of piloting (there are thousands of registered and unregistered pilots throughout the United States). If the thief himself can't fly, he can easily find a partner in crime with the necessary skills to do so, or simply abduct the owner/pilot and force him to pilot the plane to an unknown destination.

Once in the air the criminal may be requested by control towers to provide certain flight data, in addition to making periodic radio contacts. This is accomplished by providing false information, or by forcing the hijacked owner to respond with the necessary communications. Aircraft are stolen for many reasons, and an alarming number are used for illegal drug trafficking. Most are flown out of the state or even out of the country and never recovered, at least not in one piece. If the thief cannot fly or is unable to take off unnoticed, he usually steals as much of the equipment as possible. Then again, this might have been his original goal. Much equipment found in a plane can easily be removed with simple hand tools and smuggled out of airports or hangars. The thief usually removes items that offer the best chance of resale, and have the least chance of recovery by the police and/or owner.

It's not unique for a thief to steal items from one plane and switch them with another similar plane, enabling him to carry hard-to-trace equipment away from the second plane. The owner of the first plane reports the theft and the identification or serial numbers of the stolen equipment to the police. These numbers will be listed as "hot items," but will rarely turn up since they are now located in a legitimate plane.

To decrease the likelihood of theft, every aircraft owner should follow these simple steps:

- Always attempt to store aircraft inside a secure hangar or building.
- Be sure that the aircraft storage location is adequately lighted.
- If aircraft is parked outside, always lock up doors and chalk wheels. Use tie-down cable that is constructed of metal that will stand up against a certain amount of cutting.
- Never leave ignition key inside plane.
- If you must leave an extra key with airport personnel, make sure they practice proper key control.
- Make sure your aircraft has adequate insurance coverage.
- Record aircraft serial/identification numbers and affix a special identification number in a secret location on the plane. Also record engine serial number and serial numbers of related equipment.
- Never leave high-value items inside plane.
- Apply alarm systems and anti-theft devices when possible.
- Maintain up-to-date color photographs of plane and equipment.
- Do not store aircraft log book with plane.
- Inventory and check radios and navigation equipment with serial number check list to make sure they have not been switched. (Place your own identification on these items in addition to existing identification.)
- Know who works around hangars and guards your aircraft.
- Always conduct a flight check prior to take-off to make sure everything is in working order.
- Contact local police immediately if your plane has been broken into or stolen. Provide full identification of aircraft and equipment to police.

- When purchasing aircraft, be sure that all documentation is authentic.
- Be cautious of prospective passengers who request flights across borders or into unknown and secluded locations. This is a sign of possible drug or alien smuggling.

Construction Equipment

One of the fastest growing businesses today is the theft and resale of heavy construction equipment, most of which is reportedly sent out of the country, never to be identified or recovered. Listed below are some very important measures in preventing the loss of construction machinery:

1. Never park unguarded equipment overnight.
2. Always attempt to isolate equipment away from main roads and highways that make access and escape much easier.
3. Always attempt to park all equipment within a fenced site that provides adequate lighting.
4. Employ the services of a reputable guard service to provide continual security during non-working hours.
5. If a guard force cannot be obtained, install alarm systems on equipment or perimeter gates to alert you of possible theft.
6. Request police patrols to keep an eye on equipment, particularly unusually large trailers or trucks that arrive in the area during non-working hours.
7. Mark all equipment in at least two locations to provide necessary identification.
8. Park equipment in a tight formation that makes it difficult for anyone but operators to move. A tight formation usually provides only one actual avenue through which equipment can be driven. This becomes time-consuming and too risky to attempt.
9. If you intend to park heavy, trailer-mounted equipment unattended for long periods of time, as a last resort remove the trailer wheels,.
10. When possible, ask local businesses or residents to keep an eye on your equipment and report any suspicious activity to police and local construction representative. Offer to pay, if necessary. This is a cheap way to get fair protection.

understood by all. Children need to know what actions are appropriate, and especially what actions are inappropriate. Consider the following points:

- They need to know whom they can trust completely.
- They must understand the difference between games and the perverted actions of a molester.
- They must learn to respect their bodies, and that they have a right to privacy pertaining to their bodies.
- They must not fear coming to their parents and reporting an embarrassing or frightful incident, and above all the parents must listen and provide comfort and understanding. The parent's response will usually determine how the child will react.

All children, at one time or another, have made up stories about something they have become involved with. This is to be expected and should be understood to be perfectly normal. However, when a child tells a story about how Uncle Henry touched her under her dress, she should be seriously listened to. Very few children will make up a story about an incident of this nature. Granted, you don't automatically run to Uncle Henry with threats. The incident could have been innocent, such as an accidental touch while being lifted onto a lap. Sit down with the child immediately and try to get her to tell and show you exactly what Uncle Henry did that frightened her, as well as what was said. You'll have to decide whether or not the episode was innocent and what you will do about it. You may decide to talk to Uncle Henry about what happened. Maybe you will let it go for now, but keep your eyes open when Uncle Henry is around. You might decide to call the police (if these episodes have happened before and it is more serious than a simple touch), or possibly just ignore the incident if you honestly feel that the child has been mistaken and it was purely accidental. Regardless of how you choose to handle the situation, let the child know she has done the right thing by coming to you, and that you will take care of it.

Sexual assault often begins innocently, or appears innocent to a child. What starts as a playful touch can turn into a serious assault. Children seldom lie about something as scary to them as this, but it can be difficult for them to tell their parents. After being assaulted they are likely to be confused and scared when faced with the idea that:

- If they tell their mommy or daddy, the molester (possibly a close relative), will go to jail and never see them again.
- That they will be injured or killed.
- Their parents will be hurt or that they will be taken away from them and it will be all their fault.
- They feel that nobody will believe them or that no one cares.

As we have noted, the offender is often a close friend or relative. The child is supposedly safe and secure with the babysitter or Aunt Susie. For this reason the offender has continuous access to the child. In other words, don't necessarily look for the offender outside the family circle. He could well be inside. Children feel safe with relatives, but when something like this occurs they know that they will see Aunt Susie tomorrow and are afraid to talk.

Love and affection includes holding and touching. Children need this contact. Unfortunately, it can be the basis for an assault by a sick, disturbed person.

How many times have you been told to obey your elders? This alone can lead to confusion when a child is asked to keep quiet about a questionable act. "Don't tell mommy or daddy what happened. It's just between you and me." "It's just a game." This person will usually continue to abuse your child until he or she is caught.

Signals of Possible Abuse

The child becomes:
- Very frightened, experiencing nightmares, and possibly begins wetting the bed.
- Very confused, and cannot sleep.
- Less active than normal and withdraws from everyone.
- Scared to be left alone or with certain people.
- Sick or experiences irritation and pain on private areas of his or her body.
- Curious and asks unusual questions about her body or certain physical actions.
- Depressed and loses her appetite.

What to Ask Your Child

If you believe your child or another child has been abused, ask the following questions of them, or notify their parents or a trusted relative of your concerns.

- Has something strange and scary happened?
- What have they been doing?
- Who have they been with, and where?
- Have they been hurt or threatened? (Assure them it is all right to tell you.)

What to Tell Your Child

- Whom they may play with.
- Whom they can travel with.
- Who may touch or kiss them, and where.
- Who may help them go to the bathroom.
- Who may help them dress or undress.
- Who may give them food and medicine.
- Whom they may stay with overnight.
- Who may dress and undress in front of them.
- That they should inform you where they are at *all* times.
- That it is all right to say "No, I don't like that," or, "Leave me alone," to anyone making them feel uncomfortable.
- That any strange incident should be told to you, and that you are not afraid and will take care of it. (With this in mind, they will tell you almost everything that frightens them.)
- Be aware of any strangers, men or women, who ask questions or try to become friends and to tell you when it happens.
- Write down the license plate number of the car of a strange person approaching them.
- Run or stay away from strangers who offer gifts, money, or candy.
- Stay away from any of their friends getting into a stranger's car, but to get the license number and report it immediately.
- Leave anyone who gets too close and wants to touch them. They should run for help.

- Never go into strange homes or strange stores.
- Never go into a deserted area of a building.
- Never play alone.
- That they can say no to scary or frightening games. If someone persists, they should tell another adult immediately.
- Teach them to scream for help, bite, kick, and run if someone grabs them. (See Chapter 15 for detailed tactics.)

What Parents Need to Know

- The background of all household employees—the butler, maid, chauffeur, cook, babysitter, and even the once-a-week housekeeper. Be especially careful with those who have custody of your children when you are gone.
- All your children's friends. Encourage them to talk about them with you and invite them over so that you can become acquainted with them.
- Changes in your child's behavior.
- Always know where your children are, who they are with, and what they are doing.
- How important it is for their safety for both you and your children to know what threats exist, and the urgency of reporting any incident to the police.

Always try to be aware of how your own actions affect your children. For example, never force your children to hug or kiss friends or relatives if it is obvious they dislike this behavior. When you do so, you are apt to make children feel that they are not supposed to refuse an adult certain acts that make them uneasy. Yet every day parents force their children to give hugs and kisses to friends or relatives, or persuade them to sit or be held on the laps of people with whom they feel uncomfortable. What can happen is that a child's feelings become confused, and they lose confidence in themselves, often rejecting the natural urge to walk away from an adult who intends to exploit the situation.

To help children understand the difference between right and wrong, it is often necessary to discuss experiences at their level. They must understand what can harm them. They do not always need to fully understand the details, such as the difference between rape and attempted rape; they do need to be aware of which actions are considered good and which are considered bad.

What to Do if Your Child Is Assaulted

Handle each incident on a case-by-case basis. It is, however, recommended that you:

- Talk with the child and tactfully gain as many details of the incident as possible.
- Report it to the police. Merely keeping the child away from the offender allows another child to become a possible victim.
- Tell the child that he or she did the right thing by telling you.
- See your family doctor or have a medical examination immediately.
- Don't show anger. This can make the child feel at fault or guilty for telling.

Explain that you are very concerned about what has happened, and because you love them you want to help. Remind them that you are not angry and that they are not to blame! Reassure them everything is all right, and that they don't have to see this person again. If they do not want to talk with you about it, they may talk to a grandmother, or to a special friend or teacher.

Do not avoid or ignore your child's stories about any crime or dangerous act. Believe it first, then confirm it. If it is real, assure your child everything is all right and that they did right by telling you. Then report it to the police, even if it involves a relative. This is for your child's safety, and also to get medical/psychological help for the offender. If it is false, don't punish your child. Explain how serious this sort of incident can be and answer all questions posed by the child. Remind them to come to you any time they feel they are being abused, even if they could be wrong. Never scold a child for coming to you but at the same time, tactfully explain the story of "The Boy Who Cried Wolf."

For further help or information, contact:

- Your local Child Welfare Department, Social Services Organization, or Child Abuse Center, which are listed in your telephone book.

Kidnapping, Custodial Abduction, Pushouts/Throwaways and Runaways

Temporarily losing a child in a shopping center or amusement park strikes terror in the hearts of all parents. Most of these parents are fortunate in that their youngsters are quickly located. Others are not so fortunate; their children are never found. The number of minors who turn up missing in the United States is conservatively estimated to be in the neighborhood of 100,000 annually.

Newspaper reports and TV newscasts regularly carry stories of missing and murdered children. Many of these incidents are inaccurately reported; national statistics on these cases are especially misleading. It's important to be aware of the potential dangers of kidnapping, however, exaggerated claims tend to cause unnecessary worry and fear to families, especially to parents. In order to report the most accurate information possible on this topic, I have extensively researched data that have been established by authoritative sources. One of the most valuable sources available is an organization known as SEARCH.

> SEARCH publishes the National Runaway/Missing Persons Report, a magazine containing photographs, physical descriptions, and personal data on missing children, teenagers, and adults. The report goes to over twenty-five thousand individuals and agencies in law enforcement and in medical, social, and other services. All deal with the public in professions and locations dedicated to exploring the best ways to identify, report, assist, or detain those being sought. The report provides information for these professionals and serves as a support system, but does not substitute for them.

Kidnapping

One of the most misreported crimes is that of child kidnapping. Kidnapping is the seizing of a person for extortion purposes. Abduction is often confused with or related to kidnapping, but it usually takes place for reasons other than economical ones. A criminal may *kidnap* the child of a wealthy banker for ransom, but a father is likely to *abduct* his child from his divorced wife for family reasons. If you think in this context, you will be able to discern the major differences between kidnapping and abduction as you learn more about these crimes.

Although estimates of the numbers of kidnappings by strangers that occur annually in the United States range as high as 50,000, these inflated numbers are simply not true. If 50,000 children were kidnapped annually, there would be more than 137 kidnappings each day. This total would be equivalent to 220 kidnappings per million people in the United States. On a local level, it would mean:

Area Population	Kidnappings Per Year
10,000	2.2
25,000	5.5
50,000	11
100,000	22
250,000	55
500,000	110
750,000	165
1,000,000	220

When you consider what this would equate to in *your* community, you will probably agree that these figures seem far-fetched.

The nature of the crime of kidnapping immediately transforms many suspected kidnapping incidents into dramatic news stories, often before all the facts are in.

SEARCH publisher Charles Sutherland maintains that, "if all reports of the kidnappings or unexplained disappearances of children and organized crime figures were combined, a high annual rate might reach 150." He believes that pinpointing even 50 specific cases of kidnapping per year would be very difficult to do.

> "In calling attention to this totally unfounded claim of 50,000 cases, SEARCH does not dismiss the seriousness of even one case. On the contrary. Rare as these situations may be, each creates horror, massive reactions, and emotional scars that will never vanish. Even when a child has been recovered, the psychological damages do not disappear with the solution of the case."

Custodial Abductions or Child Snatchings

In these cases, a child is taken away from one parent by another. According to SEARCH, anywhere from 25,000 to 100,000 children are snatched by separated or divorced parents annually. These figures were developed by The American Bar Association and a group called Children's Rights, Inc., both of Washington, D.C., and are considered highly accurate, but the differential of 75,000 cases is strong evidence of the lack of truly accurate statistics.

Faced with this gap in reliable data, many media people regularly cite the top-end figure of 100,000. An additional complicating factor in compiling these data is that few cases are reviewed to see if custody has actually been granted. In over half of the custody snatchings, the so-called abduction takes place before the courts have awarded custody to a parent. Therefore, no law has been broken.

Custody laws differ from state to state, as do the penalties for their violations. In SEARCH's view,

> "Until more uniform statistics exist, this state-to-state variation in applicable codes will present serious problems. In states with weak codes, law enforcement personnel have nothing to work with. Legislation must come first."

The Non-Snatched Snatched Child

What happens when the court-appointed parent (custodial parent) leaves the area with the child, depriving the other parent of visitation rights? Legally there is little that can be done to rectify this situation. The non-custodial parent is left stranded and forced to locate his or her child alone, an expensive undertaking in time, money, and emotional wear and tear. If and when the child is located, there still are no useful legal avenues for the non-custodial parent.

In too many cases, the children suffer terribly from the actions of their parents, rarely understanding what is happening, or why. All they know is that Mom and Dad are not together and they are forced to choose between one or the other. In most cases, the courts choose for them. In some cases, they are moved around the country by one parent to escape from the other parent. Nobody wins. Any way you look at it, the children are the ones who lose.

Pushouts or Throwaways

Very few people will recognize the words "pushout," or "throwaway." These labels are given to children who are forced to leave their homes by their parents, children who are abandoned, or who are literally dumped on the streets. Many are exiled for life, never to be welcomed home. They represent the single most unaccounted-for group of children in the United States—some 500,000 cases annually. It is estimated that approximately 35 percent of these children come from divorced families in which neither parent wants them.

Pushouts and throwaways do not become part of the usual statistics mentioned in studies or surveys. These unfortunate children tend not to be reported as missing by their parents. More often than not, parents claim that the child is away visiting distant grandparents or has been enrolled at an out-of-state private school. Sometimes these children are reported as runaways. How many so-called runaway children are actually forced to leave home? What pressures force them to leave?

Although each case must be weighed on its own merits, the following reasons are representative of the majority of cases reported:

- Divorce or separation of parents, resulting in neither parent wanting the child.
- Remarriage of one parent, whereupon the new spouse refuses to accept and care for a child from the previous marriage.
- The child becomes involved with drugs, alcohol, or crime. The parent is unable or unwilling to deal with the child and forces him or her to leave.
- The parent becomes involved with drugs, alcohol, or crime, forcing the child to handle responsibilities prematurely. When the child makes a mistake, the parent cannot cope and forces the child to leave.
- The parents are unable or unwilling to handle normal childhood problems as they occur, which intensifies the problems as the child grows up.
- The parents fail to provide love, affection, and discipline by being too busy to become closely involved with their children. Parents go one way, children go another. The first sign of trouble leads to a major family crisis, forcing the child to accept possibly unreasonable demands and thus, forcing him to leave.
- The children are given too much freedom, and the lack of responsibility leads to involvement with social problems (drugs, crime, etc.). Last-minute attempts by parents to regain control over the child fail and the child runs wild, and is eventually forced to leave.

Many adults who grew up with radical philosophies that stressed "individual freedoms," "escaping" from the establishment, or "finding yourself," often with the help of drugs, have allowed this philosophy to affect their childraising practices, with predictable results. The 1970s produced the largest number of throwaway children to date. This increase in throwaways also appears to have been directly related to the high divorce rate of the 1970s.

Will the U.S. throwaway rate decrease? Social change, increasing parental acceptance of responsibility, and lower overall birth rates, are expected to contribute to a decline. Meanwhile, however, uncounted numbers of children will be raised by welfare systems, foster homes, and institutions. Many will fall into a life of crime, and then to a life in prison. The final tragic chapter in many of these young people's lives will be suicide.

Runaways

The largest group of missing children are the "runaways." Approximately 1,150,000 runaway incidents, or "episodes," take place each year. SEARCH defines episodes as the number of incidents involving a runaway child, not just the number of children who have run away. Some children run away more than once. The organization has devised an accurate formula for determining the number of runaway episodes a particular location can expect: In a region with a fairly substantial population, one-half of one percent of the total number of people will roughly equal the number of runaway episodes annually. (In less densely populated areas, this formula may be inaccurate.)

Based on a total U.S. population of 230,000,000, this formula translates to 1,150,000 runaway episodes per year. Ninety percent of all runaways return home within a 14-day period, most within 48 hours. The remaining (missing) 10 percent become closed cases and the child is written off as a stay-away runner.

Why do kids run away? Many will tell you that it is because they are unhappy or that they fear their parents' reaction to some unpleasant news. The fact is, a happy child, one who is contented with life, will not run away. Perhaps the family is moving out of state and the child feels strongly opposed to it; or maybe a child is forced to quit a sports program in order to spend more time on school studies. Other more serious reasons, such as divorce or separation of the parents, can spark a child's departure. Unlike the case of the pushout, this child has the option of returning home.

Long-term runaways constitute a significant proportion of the total. Some may become involved in illegal activity and consider it impossible to return home. Others may have become active in cults, and find it difficult to escape. Though cult statistical data is unavailable, membership in one of the many cult organizations across the country is possible, and could account for a large number of missing children.

It is important to be realistic in examining this national problem. To report on and discuss runaways it is necessary to weigh the number who return home against the number who leave. To do less is a gross misrepresentation of the total problem.

How to Locate and Identify Your Child

If your child were to disappear, could you provide timely, accurate information to the police and other agencies that could help locate him or her? Being prepared is extremely important to you and your children. It doesn't cost much, and takes little time.

SEARCH recommends the following ways to provide the accurate information necessary to locate and identify a child. Each child in your home should have his or her own complete portfolio containing information that can quickly and accurately identify them.

- Photograph your children every six months, particularly during their growing years. Any type of photograph will do, providing it contains clear, sharp, facial details. Try to avoid cluttered backgrounds.
- Weigh and measure your children on the same schedule. Include height, weight, clothing and shoe size on the back of the current photo.
- Fingerprint your children. Simply buy a stamp pad with black ink and some plain 3 × 5 index cards. That is all you need. It will be a little messy and probably take several tries before you get usable prints for both hands. But you can and must do this. Don't expect local law enforcement agencies to do it for you, although more and more have taken on this task.
- Determine where all medical records can be located, particularly any x-rays of injuries. Learn how long this material will be kept on file. Storage time may be limited and you must obtain this material prior to its destruction or before you move to a distant location. You have every right to this material. Insist that you get it.
- Treat dental x-rays and records in exactly the same way.
- Try to learn specific blood type. This information may be available through testing done in connection with other

medical procedures. Check with all physicians involved in treating your children. Some high school teenagers may know their blood type through advanced biology course work.

- If allergies or other conditions require prescription medication, learn the names of the medications, their required schedule of use, and dosages to be taken. Determine the effects if not taken as prescribed.
- Record the size, description, and location of moles, warts, scars, tattoos, and birthmarks.
- If the child wears eyeglasses, obtain prescription data and frame types for all pairs. Know the type and prescription of contact lenses.
- Consult with school personnel to determine any specific disabilities or achievements (in many systems, "Special Education" describes both gifted children and those with learning problems). Sources for this information will vary somewhat according to grade level and school system. Know your child's class placement (sometimes called "Track Level"). If in any doubt about details, ask questions and get specifics.
- Does the child have any distinctive characteristics of speech or behavior? Remember, what you take for granted may be considered quite distinctive to an individual or agency in its efforts to help find a missing youngster.

These recommendations were designed with children in mind, but can easily be used to develop a portfolio on adults as well. Every member of your family should be able to be identified immediately. Adult portfolios should include information such as the following:

- Driver's license number, social security number, medicare number, and any other identifying forms of identification.
- Hobbies, pastimes, or activities and the locations the individual frequents.

If Your Child Is Missing

Always immediately report facts and circumstances to the police. Provide them with complete information on your missing child. Tell them all you know about the disappearance, including family conflict that could have sparked this behavior or any motive or reason for your spouse to abduct your child.

Request immediate inclusion of the case in the FBI-operated National Crime Information Center computer for national availability of information. This can normally be done through your local police or sheriff's office. If not, contact your nearest FBI office with this request—they are obligated to list all missing children on their computer. Do not hire outside services, order posters printed, call a missing persons bureau or organization, or take any other action until you have discussed it with your local law enforcement agency. A "panic button" reaction, and the feeling that you have to do something is natural, but may not necessarily be helpful. Your local police agency may be limited in size, but its capacity for communication far exceeds yours.

Tips for Parents

The following information can help prevent your child from being taken from you for any reason. Parents, educate your children. Warn them of the possibility that they could be taken away from you, or assaulted. It is no game, and definitely is not fun. Inform them that they should:

- Under no circumstances associate with strangers.
- Never talk with strangers.
- Never accept gifts from strangers.
- Never go near a stranger's car.
- Never leave their parents for even one second without them knowing exactly where they are.
- Never hitchhike.
- Never walk alone, but always with a friend, and in the light.
- Never invite a stranger into their home.
- Never answer questions asked by a stranger over the telephone or in person, even if they tell them, "It's okay, your daddy/mommy know me."
- Never take shortcuts to or from school.
- Stay away from deserted buildings, dark alleyways, and secluded areas, including doorways of abandoned buildings.
- Never enter abandoned buildings.
- Always tell their parents exactly where they will be, for how long, and when they will return.

- Quickly run for help if they think someone is trying to trick them, or get them to come with them.
- Report all important information to their parents and police immediately.
- Tell the police and their parents immediately if they see a friend being forced into the car of a stranger.
- Scream and yell as loud as possible that they are being kidnapped if they are grabbed. If the stranger does not let go, then bite, kick, and run. (See Chapter 15.)
- Try to remain calm if they are taken away by a stranger. Remember, their parents will call the police when they find they are missing. Wait for a good opportunity to break free and run. When they are around other people, call for help, yelling their name and address. If they can escape safely, then immediately get help. Run into a store or among another family and tell them that someone is trying to hurt them, and that they want to call the police.

It is very important to help your children become aware that there are bad people out in the world, but it is just as important that they know there are good people who will help them, too. Do not place too much responsibility on your children. Sometimes parents feel that once they have told their children what to do and what not to do, everything will be fine. Don't count on this. Children can be easily tricked. Consider how confused your child could become in the following situations.

A stranger tells Susie that he works with Mommy and that she has asked him to please pick her up from school for her. A stranger tells Johnny that he is a relative (aunt, uncle, cousin) who just arrived today for a surprise visit and has permission to pick him up from school to get to know him better, and wouldn't it be fun to stop for an ice cream cone on the way home? What about a stranger who says he knows Superman (or any other superhero, or even a TV or movie star), and wouldn't Bobby like to meet him?

Children are very impressionable, and if someone wants your child badly enough, for whatever reason, he will use any means he can think of to accomplish his task. Teaching your children how to react to strangers is important. Realizing that any child can become a victim, and always remembering it, is just as important.

Child Find, Inc. is another organization that is nationally recognized for its work with missing children. This nonprofit organization's primary objective is to "help parent and child victims of child snatchings by establishing a central registration point for matching separated children and their searching parents."

Child Find's major goal is to inform the missing child that:

1. There is an address and telephone number to use in making contact with lost parents.
2. There are other children who face similar problems.
3. Parents do care and are searching for them.
4. It is okay to make contact with a lost parent.

To contact *Child Find*, write or call:

Child Find, Inc.
P.O. Box 277
New Paltz, New York 12561-0277
(914) 255-1848
(800) 431-5005 This number is reserved for use by children.
Gloria J. Yerkovich, *Director*
Kristin Cole Brown, *Information Director*

To contact *Search* write or call:

Search
ATTN: Charles A. Sutherland, *Publisher*
560 Sylvan Avenue
Englewood Cliffs, New Jersey 07632
(201) 567-4040 general information.

Search recommends the following reading:

- *The Runaways: Children, Wives, Husbands & Parents,* Myron Brenton, Little, Brown & Co. *(Hardcover),* Penguin Books *(Paperback)*
- *The Social Psychology of Runaways,* Timothy Brennan, Lexington Books *(Hardcover)*
- *Parental Child-Stealing,* Michael W. Agopian, Lexington Books *(Hardcover)*
- *America's Runaways,* Christine Chapman, William Morrow & Co. *(Hardcover)*
- *Child Abuse & Neglect,* H. Glavretto, Ballinger Publications *(Hardcover)*

Muggers and Purse Snatchers and Pickpockets

No book on crime prevention would be complete without a look at three of the most frequently committed personal crimes; muggings, purse-snatchings, and pickpocketing.

The Mugger

The mugger relies on the use of force or the threat of violence to get what he is after. The crime he commits is *personal robbery*. Personal robbery differs from purse-snatching and pickpocketing in that they are crimes of *personal larceny*. In the case of larceny, no threat of force exists between the criminal and his intended victim.

In most cases, the mugger stalks his prey alone. On some occasions, though, he may solicit the aid of a female accomplice (or vice versa) to persuade an unsuspecting victim to retreat to her room or a deserted alleyway. Close behind, the mugger(s) enters, and strips the victim of all valuables. If lucky, the victim escapes uninjured. If he struggles or resists, the mugger is likely to beat him, many times into unconsciousness. Muggers often carry weapons and are not afraid to use them. Since a mugger survives on force, the possession of a weapon is a necessity.

The targets these criminals choose all have certain characteristics in common. They may be new to the area and appear lost or confused, or they may exhibit weaknesses such as a lack of confidence or the inability to protect themselves. Obvious victims are the drunks and the drug addicts sleeping unprotected in alleyways or on park benches. But the ordinary citizen can fall victim as well. Just as the mugger chooses his **victims** carefully, he is careful when choosing **locations** to commit his evil deeds. Dark doorways or hallways, abandoned buildings, elevators, and parks all pose a real threat to the lone passerby. Once a victim is grabbed (usually from behind), the mugger forcefully searches his pockets for money and pulls any jewelry from arms, hands, ears, and around the neck. Some victims pay dearly when rings or earrings fail to slide off easily. Cut fingers and torn ear lobes are not uncommon. In several instances, fingers have been cut off to remove rings.

Once the criminal feels satisfied that anything of value is now in his own pockets, he quickly disappears down a convenient alleyway. Do not follow him. Notify police immediately, providing the best description you can manage, and don't get your hopes up about recovering your valuables. Statistics are against you.

The Purse-Snatcher

A purse-snatcher can be a ten-year-old lad or a sixty-year-old granddad. The only criterion is that the thief be able to grab a

140

purse, briefcase, or other package from the arms of his victim and run quickly into concealment. Unlike the mugger, who carefully chooses the time and location for his crime, the purse-snatcher works during the day and during the night, indoors or out. Like the mugger, he too has planned his escape carefully. Once money or other valuables are removed from the snatched purse or case, it is usually discarded.

The purse-snatcher is apt to work alone, targeting bus stops, shopping centers, crowded sidewalks, and other highly traveled areas filled with likely victims. He chooses his victims like a mugger would, approaching only those that he believes will not chase him or offer any resistance. Once his meal ticket is spotted, he springs into action, catching his victim off guard.

There are three "methods" of purse-snatching. The "bag or purse opener" is more like a pickpocket. He spots his intended victim, follows, then attempts to open the purse and surreptitiously steal anything he can get his fingers on. The second and third methods are similar, with the exception of the snatch itself. The "clipper," as he is commonly called, cuts or "clips" the strap of the purse free from his victim with a knife or razor; the other "snatcher" simply jerks and pulls it free. These techniques can injure the victim, especially if a struggle ensues.

The Pickpocket

Probably the most sophisticated of all "personal" thieves is the professional pickpocket who is usually endowed with skilled hands and techniques that include using a newspaper or a hanky as major tools of his trade.

The pickpocket generally operates on crowded streets, inside shopping plazas, and at recreational centers, as well as on public transportation. The crowded bus or subway allows the pickpocket to get very close to his victim without raising a lot of suspicion. Many pickpockets work the streets alone, but more than a few professionals require the aid of one or two partners. In these cases, the pickpocket, commonly called the "mechanic," selects his intended victim and signals to his assistant. The assistant, known as the "stall," then distracts the target by falling into him or pushing him, always responding with an apology. At that exact moment, the mechanic lifts or picks the victim's wallet and passes it to a third accomplice who remains in the same position to avoid raising suspicion.

Because of the length of time required to master the skills of a pickpocket, and because much of the cash once found in wallets is being replaced by credit cards, this profession is slowly dying out.

How To Avoid These Threats

- Walk confidently and look alert.
- Never carry large sums of money or expensive jewelry on your person.
- Never keep all your money, checks, and credit cards in the same purse or pocket. Spread them out, and, if possible, leave them home. *Note:* Be sure to record the serial numbers of all credit cards, checks, licenses, and other important documents, and keep this list in a safe place at home or in a safe deposit box.
- Carry your wallet in a front pocket or at least in one where you would be able to feel it being removed.
- Carry your purse or briefcase on the side of your body nearest traffic.
- Carry your purse tightly under your arm, keeping the straps secured around your arm. If possible, carry a purse without a strap.
- Never leave your purse or packages unguarded in a shopping cart or on a park bench while shopping, unloading groceries, or waiting for a bus or taxi.
- Plan your route thoroughly.
- Travel with a companion when at all possible.
- Take your dog along on a leash.

If Your Purse or Briefcase Is Grabbed:

- Never engage in a wrestling match, and never chase after the thief. He may have a weapon and turn on you. Instead, report the incident to the police immediately, providing as much of a description as possible. Also, attempt to get witnesses who observed the incident to provide a statement to the police.

As a last resort, if you are being followed or you feel you are likely to be attacked, toss your valuables into a United States Mail Box or even a garbage bin. Most criminals will not take the time to dig them out. Don't forget to contact the police and the Post Office immediately to regain your property.

Senior Citizens

The physical limitations of Americans 65 or older make them, as a group, as susceptible to crime as children. In contrast, the Bureau of Justice Statistics Bulletin reports that senior citizens are less likely to be victimized.

These statistics may reflect their growing fear of venturing outside their homes, where they are most vulnerable to criminal activities.

When victimized, the elderly experience considerable fear and panic even when not physically injured. The economic effects of crime also make an enormous impact on senior citizens, and in many instances they are forced to take expensive precautionary measures. These forces combine to severely curtail their lifestyles and limit their freedom.

Today's 24 million senior citizens constitute approximately one-tenth of the U.S. population. Their numbers are growing rapidly as life spans lengthen; it is estimated that by the year 2000 the elderly will make up more than 20 percent of the population.

For the most part, the elderly individual is more likely to be personally victimized during daylight, in open public places, than at any other time and or in any other location. Yet contrary to popular belief, 86 percent of all personal crime experienced by the elderly consisted of personal larcenies without contact, and only 14 percent of the crimes included purse-snatching and pickpocketing. This 14 percent figure reflects a serious problem when it involves injury. Since larceny is the major crime against the elderly, it is particularly important for senior citizens to take steps to secure their homes against crime.

Precautions to Take:

- Keep important documents and valuables such as jewelry and coin collections secured inside a safe deposit box at your bank. Make sure that a relative or friend is aware of this in order to help you in the event of an emergency. Never allow access to a stranger.
- Have social security checks and other income deposited directly into your bank account.

- Know the employees at your bank and establish a friendly relationship with them.
- Never answer questions over the telephone about your activities, financial status, family, etc.
- If a person calls attempting to verify your financial status by stating he represents your bank, do not provide answers. No legitimate bank verifies accounts this way.
- Never agree to enter into an insurance or medical program without first verifying its authenticity.
- If you are robbed or assaulted, always report it immediately.
- Many communities have formed groups to help senior citizens reduce the risk of crime. Try to locate one near you.

How To Avoid Crime

- Always travel with a friend.
- Always leave a light on at home when you go out.
- Never enter your home if it looks like it may have been broken into. Call the police from a neighbor's.
- Ask a friend to escort you home, especially in a high-crime area, or ask the taxi driver to help you into your home.
- Never argue if approached or surprised by a criminal. Never argue, but submit to all demands.
- Never carry all your money in one purse or in your wallet.
- Never carry a large purse. Try not to carry one at all.
- Never place your wallet in your back pocket.
- Never flash your money.
- Stay away from deserted parks, buildings, and streets.
- Never go near bushes or dark doorways.
- Always walk in lighted areas.
- Never board a bus or train if it is empty.
- Never go into dark parking lots or garages alone.

Families should take more interest in the safety and well-being of their elderly members. Explain potential problems to them and help them to secure their homes against intruders. Provide transportation to and from the store on a regular basis.

Too often, the elderly are forgotten after working hard all their lives and struggling to raise their families. They are often left alone in a subsidized apartment, where their recreation may be limited to watching television or feeding the pigeons. We all need to take more time to love, care for, and protect our senior citizens. They need it and deserve it. It won't be all that long until we find ourselves using our senior citizen discount cards.

For more information on crime prevention for the elderly, contact your local police department or:

- National Council of Senior Citizens
  1511 K Street, NW
  Washington, DC 20005
- American Association of Retired Persons/
  National Retired Teachers Association
  1909 K Street, NW
  Washington, DC 20049

Submission vs. Resistance: Balancing the Scales

What should you do if you're grabbed and forced to hand over your purse? There's no simple answer. Anyone who quickly tells you exactly how to react to a very threatening situation either gets his information from a crystal ball or really has not taken enough time to evaluate the matter. The possibilities are numerous.

As I have continually stressed, avoid threatening situations whenever possible. But even with planned prevention on your side, the possibilities of facing a criminal, for whatever reason, are there. Depending on the circumstances, (mugging, robbery, rape, etc.), some situations require immediate defensive tactics. For example: Three thugs stop you and say they feel like breaking a few bones because they haven't broken any this week. There is very little talking that will keep them from carrying out their threat, though it wouldn't hurt to give it a try. Unfortunately, you probably can't offer them your wallet, because they're likely to have taken it anyway.

As a rule, if avoidance doesn't work, obey all of the criminal's demands. Remember, you are the only one who can evaluate the situation. As you are complying with the demands, you might decide that your best chance of escaping injury or death is through total cooperation. This is usually the most recommended strategy to follow. However, you may decide to talk calmly with the assailant(s), and use verbal resistance to talk your way out of the situation. Verbal resistance *does not* mean yelling, shouting, or arguing with your assailant. This may and probably will make him even more nervous and cause him to injure you to quiet you. This *does* mean to verbally provide comments that might make him change his mind, such as, "Let's talk this over," "It's not too late to give this up and run," or "You are only making it tough on yourself." In the case of a rapist, some people recommend saying that you have VD or herpes, but be aware that this could backfire on you. If this guy is six-foot-four, weighs 280 pounds, and is emotionally intent on raping you, telling him you have VD might get him so upset that he will beat you in frustration. Self-prevention is the first law of nature, but remember, nothing says that you cannot reach the same goal of survival by submitting—by giving in to demands.

However, if after analyzing the situation thoroughly, you still feel that you're in for major injuries and there's a chance of getting killed, it's time to take that last chance for survival, and apply defensive/offensive tactics to overpower your aggressor. Once you have made your decision to resist, what you *will* do is largely determined by what you *can* do. Increase your options by remaining calm, and thinking clearly. The more options you have, the better the chances of surviving without injury. You may even be able to escape.

Your ability to remain calm is based on how prepared you are to face a threatening situation. Don't think for a moment that because you are prepared you won't be scared. Police officers and U.S. military personnel, some of the best-trained people in the world, will readily acknowledge being scared during a conflict. The difference is that they are trained to control fear by recognizing that it's a normal emotional reaction, and that through careful training they will do what has to be done to accomplish their mission. So can you.

Weigh Loss/Gain Factors

There are several points to consider first, and one of them is who else may be with you. If your wife or children are with you when you are robbed, your options are limited. The best bet, again, is to give in to demands, because if a struggle begins, your wife or children may also be injured. If you are the only one threatened, you can always run, but not when your entire family is held hostage. It's time to weigh the losses versus the gains. The safety of your family is the most important consideration.

CHAPTER ELEVEN

Compensating Victims of Violent Crimes

According to the Department of Justice, from 1982-1983, one out of every three families in the United States will be a victim of crime. For many, many years, emphasis was placed on the rehabilitation of criminals, with little or no thought given to compensation for the victims of their crimes. Currently, 37 states and the District of Columbia actively support these victims and enable them, or their surviving dependents to be eligible for certain benefits. Compensation varies from state to state. As a rule, however, victims are able to place a claim for medical expenses, drug and rehabilitative expenses, physical or mental disabilities, funeral expenses, loss of past or future wage earnings, loss of support for family dependents, loss of family members (such as child care provided by a mother), attorney's fees, and, in some cases, property loss or damage.

Most states require that to be eligible to receive benefits the victim must:

1. Not be related to the offender or maintain a close or intimate relationship with him or her.
2. Not have provoked the incident or become a victim due to wrongful conduct.
3. Not have become injured through an unintentional motor vehicle accident.
4. Report the crime to the police within 72 hours.
5. Apply for benefits within one year of the incident.

The offender does not have to be arrested for a victim or victim's dependents to collect benefits. Most states will also provide these benefits regardless of the financial status of the victim; however, some states do require that a need for such benefits exists or that an undue hardship exists.

All participating states have established a set maximum amount of benefits that can be received. These limits though, do not always apply to certain claims, such as medical expenses to elderly victims, or victims disabled by injuries received during the claimed violent crime.

As indicated on the following chart, each state has a filing deadline, which must be met. Once the request for benefits is filed, a victim can expect to wait anywhere from one to 30 months, although almost all states provide emergency funds, which are usually available immediately upon request. Some of these emergency funds have set limits ($500 to $1,500), and others have no limits at all. Maximum benefits awarded can range anywhere from $1,500 to $50,000.

Thirteen states do not currently (as of the publication of this book) award benefits, but it is reasonable to assume that they will eventually adopt this program.

Victim Compensation Programs

State	Telephone Number	Maximum Award	Maximum Emergency Award	Filing Deadline
Alaska	907-465-3040	$40,000	$1,500	2 years
California	916-322-4426	$23,000	$1,000	1 year
Colorado	303-575-5176	$ 1,500	$ 500	6 months
Connecticut	203-566-4156	$10,000	$ 500	2 years
Delaware	302-571-3030	$10,000	No limit	1 year
District of Columbia	202-724-3936	$25,000	$1,000	6 months
Florida	904-488-0848	$10,000	$ 500	1 year
Hawaii	808-548-4680	$10,000	No	18 months
Illinois	312-793-2585	$15,000	No	6 months
Indiana	317-232-3808	$10,000	$ 500	3 months
Iowa	515-281-5044	$ 2,000	$ 500	6 months
Kansas	913-296-2359	$10,000	No limit	1 year
Kentucky	502-564-2290	$15,000	$ 500	1 year
Louisiana	504-342-6740	$50,000	$ 500	1 year
Maryland	301-523-5000	$45,000	$1,000	6 months
Massachusetts	617-727-5025	$10,000	No	1 year
Michigan	517-373-7373	$15,000	No	1 year
Minnesota	612-296-7080	$25,000	Yes	1 year
Missouri	314-751-4231	$10,000	$ 100	1 year
Montana	406-449-2047	$25,000	No	1 year
Nebraska	402-471-2828	$10,000	$ 500	2 years
Nevada	702-885-4065	$ 5,000	No	1 year
New Jersey	201-648-2107	$25,000	$1,500	2 years
New Mexico	505-841-4694	$12,500	No	1 year
New York	212-587-5160	$20,000	$1,500	1 year
North Dakota	701-224-2700	$25,000	$1,000	1 year
Ohio	614-466-7190	$25,000	No limit	1 year
Oklahoma	405-521-2330	$10,000	$ 500	1 year
Oregon	503-378-5348	$23,000	$1,000	6 months
Pennsylvania	717-783-5153	$25,000	$1,000	1 year
Rhode Island	401-277-3266	$25,000	No	2 years
South Carolina	803-758-8940	$10,000	$1,500	6 months
Tennessee	615-741-2734	$10,000	$ 500	1 year
Texas	512-475-8362	$50,000	$1,500	6 months
Virginia	804-786-5171	$10,000	$1,000	6 months
Washington	206-753-6318	$15,000	No	1 year
West Virginia	304-348-3470	$20,000	No	2 years
Wisconsin	608-266-6470	$10,000	$ 500	2 years

CHAPTER TWELVE

Domestic Violence: Child and Spouse Abuse

Mary Anne was arrested and charged with the shooting death of her husband Frank. He had been drunk all week and had been beating her, and she feared for her life. Vowing he would never let him come near her again, she got the shotgun out of the hall closet and "stopped him once and for all." Her neighbors watched as the officers led her out of the house. They had been concerned about the loud arguments next door, but no one had called the authorities.

The home is the heart of America. Strong family relationships contribute greatly to a society. Thus far, we have studied external threats that can affect the family. Now we look at the threats that are created within the home itself: family violence.

According to a 1976 FBI Uniform Crime Report, 29 percent of child murders are committed by parents, in the home. Thirty-five percent are committed by acquaintances, and 26 percent are not specifically identified. Surprisingly, only 10 percent of child murders are attributed to strangers.

Although family (domestic) violence is not new, extensive reporting of it has only come about in recent years. In the past, fear of legal retaliation for false complaints kept many neighbors from reporting abuse. Now, however, no one can be prosecuted for reporting abuse in good faith. We all have a moral responsibility to report abuse, but our legal status on this issue varies from state to state. Most laws do require that physicians, nurses, teachers, and police personnel report any suspected abuse of children and spouses.

Child Abuse

Child abuse is the continued mistreatment and/or the willful, but not always intended, neglect of children by the person(s) legally responsible for them. Abuse can lead to physical or emotional injury, and death.

In the minds of many, child abuse is limited to **physical abuse** in the form of beatings. But physical abuse can include being deprived of physical needs such as food, water, adequate shelter and clothing, and proper sanitary conditions.

Emotional abuse is usually the result of physical abuse. It can also be a single form of abuse such as neglect—the lack of love, attention, understanding, discipline, and supervision. **Verbal abuse** is closely related to emotional abuse since it has an important effect on a child's emotions. Telling the child he is no good or criticizing him too strongly are instances of emotional abuse. Other examples:

- Treating a child differently from other children in the home.
- Constantly blaming a child for problems.
- Terrifying a child with threats.
- Not showing interest in a child's activities.

Sexual abuse is probably the least-talked-about abuse, but one of the most serious. A sexually abused child may:

- Show signs of pain when sitting or walking.
- Become a problem child (use drugs, stay out of school, run away, vandalize, etc.).
- Prefer to be alone, away from children of his or her own age.

This abuse may develop under many conditions; when a large family lives in a small, crowded home, when a parent is involved with drugs or alcohol, or when one parent is constantly away from home, for example.

Any one of or a combination of these different types of child abuse can be found in over one million homes each year. As many as 2,000 children die each year as the result of abuse. The children who survive abuse are likely to carry physical and emotional scars for the rest of their lives. Many will suffer so severely that they turn to crime, or drug, and alcohol abuse. Unfortunately, children who have been abused often grow up to become parents who abuse.

152

Who Abuses Children and Why?

Abuse is found at all levels of society. Many parents who abuse their children were abused as children themselves, and it may not be just one parent, but both. The major cause of abuse can be linked to:

- Financial situation at home. Unemployment, or the inability to pay bills, places intense pressure and stress on one or both parents. When parents can't provide for their family they feel bad themselves, and emotional flare-ups lead to acts of abuse.
- The immature parent who cannot handle family crises. This can include the parent who sets unreasonable goals for children to reach and maintain.
- Emotional problems caused by stress or illness, and childhood problems suffered by the parent.
- Drug and alcohol abuse or addiction.

Generally, most abusive parents do not suffer from some strange affliction, but are, in fact, quite normal. Very few are emotionally or mentally disturbed.

Sometimes parents fail to realize their abusive tendencies. To them, everything is fine, or they keep repeating, "I won't do it again." Once they realize that a problem does exist, many cry out for help. They don't want to risk losing their families, but they must acknowledge the problem, and take the necessary steps to get help. The only way many recognize their abuse is when they seriously injure a child or are reported by a neighbor, friend, or relative.

Child abusers can be helped. They can learn to recognize the problem and eliminate it. If they are willing to make the effort, 90 percent of abusive parents can be successfully treated.

Although I have talked about parents as abusers, children can be abused by friends or relatives. Look for the following signs:

- Child fears parent, guardian, sibling, or friend.
- Outgoing and friendly child suddenly withdraws from society or becomes very shy.
- Child shows signs of repeated injuries such as bruises, welts, scars, burns, broken bones, lacerations, etc.
- Child's family is isolated or unfriendly; does not associate with others and seems to be "hiding" something.

- Children who always appeared normal begin to exhibit unusual behavior (become disruptive or untrusting).
- Children who begin to appear neglected, who are under-nourished, have dirty clothing, are often left alone, or are totally unsupervised.

Few children will voluntarily ask for help or report their abuse. They attempt to hide injuries to protect their parents because they feel they deserved to be punished. Some feel it's a family matter and nobody else's business. Even in abusive households, strong ties exist, and fear of the possibilities of family breakup can be a factor keeping the child from reporting abuse. Unfortunately, they fail to realize that the abuse will continue until someone reports it or until they are seriously injured or forced to run away.

If a child wants help but is afraid to ask for it or unsure of getting it, he should go to a school counselor, minister, or anyone he feels he can trust. An abused child needs counseling just as much as the abuser does. He must be able to ask questions without fear of retaliation.

Reporting Abuse

If you're considering reporting a person you suspect is an abusive parent, you have probably gathered a substantial amount of evidence to support your suspicions. Remember that every parent at one time or another might be mistakenly labeled an abusive parent if seen spanking his or her child. Use common sense. There is a difference between punishment and severe beatings. Try to confirm your facts to prevent an inaccurate report, but do not hesitate to contact the authorities if the child's life is in immediate danger.

Usually, the agency to contact regarding child abuse is your local welfare department. When reporting abuse, provide the following information to assist in the investigation:

- Name, age, and address of the child you suspect is being abused.
- Name and address of the parent or other individual suspected of the abuse.
- When you first noticed the abuse, including circumstances, etc.
- Reason you suspect child is being abused.

- Your name, if possible. This allows the investigating agency to question you in more detail later. You can, however, remain anonymous.

Warning Signs—Before Baby is Born

Some families exhibit abusive tendencies. The following warning signs do not mean that a particular family will abuse their children, only that the possibility of abuse is there.

- A prospective mother or father does not want the baby.
- The mother or father refuses to prepare for the baby.
- The parents are overly concerned about the sex of the baby.
- The parents feel that the baby will crowd them, or limit their freedom.
- The mother is not concerned about her health or the baby's safety during pregnancy.
- The parents wanted an abortion but decided against it, remaining confused.
- The parents are considering placing the child up for adoption.

After the baby is born, if the parents show constant irritation at his cries and needs, or have nothing good to say about the baby, his future may be in jeopardy.

Asking for Help

Being a parent is difficult. The pressures associated with parenting may sometimes become too much, and the mother or father reaches a breaking point. If you begin to feel like you can't take it anymore, you may be in danger of becoming an abusive parent. The time to seek help is before you start hurting your family. Don't lose control or you could lose a child! Consider:

- Talking with your spouse, or other close relative.
- Talking with a close friend.
- Talking with a representative of your religious faith.
- Talking with a social services/welfare counselor.
- Contacting Parents Anonymous; National Center for the Prevention and Treatment of Child Abuse.

Sometimes family separations for temporary periods can help tremendously by giving everyone a chance to seriously consider the alternatives. In some cases, permanent separation is called for.

What Happens When a Report is Made?

When you report your suspicions to the local welfare or police authorities, an investigation is initiated to determine the circumstances and accuracy of the report. The Welfare Department is usually responsible for the initial investigation, and in most cases is required to submit a report of its investigation to local law enforcement authorities.

If the investigative agency finds evidence of abuse they will refer the case to the court systems. If no evidence is obtained, the case will be closed or referred to another agency that can counsel the family about a possible problem.

If the court becomes involved, then it generally will order temporary placement of the child with an agency responsible for child care while a determination of future custody can be made. The main purpose of this is to protect the child until circumstances are corrected and the child can return home.

If the court determines that the parents cannot or will not assume responsibility for providing a home setting that is healthy and an emotionally stable environment for the child to grow up in, parental rights may be terminated. In this case, the child would probably be placed for adoption, but these cases are extreme. The court prefers to return children to their parents following successful counseling and treatment.

If the court feels that there is a problem of abuse, but that it can be worked out within the family, it will place the child under the protection of the court, but allow the child to remain at home if the parent(s) agrees to participate in classes designed to end abuse. When treatment is completed, the parent(s) and program's success is evaluated. If the court finds that sufficient improvement has taken place, the family may return to a normal lifestyle. If the parent cannot cope and conform to this program, the court may then terminate parental rights and place the child up for adoption. The good news, as we have noted, is that 90 percent of abusing parents can correct their problems and regain custody of the child.

Spouse Abuse

Although it gets less attention than child abuse, spouse abuse is one of the most frequent but least-reported crimes facing today's family. It has been estimated that one out of seven women is abused by her husband, but most cases go unreported for fear that the family will break up.

Spouse abuse often leads to serious injury or death. Police officers report that responding to a domestic disturbance such as spouse abuse may be the most dangerous situation they face on the job.

Between 1976 and 1980, 32 percent of assaults on law enforcement officers were reported to have occurred while they were responding to domestic disturbances.

Women's rights groups across the country are placing more and more importance on legal support in prosecution of these cases. They charge that many police departments classify spouse abuse as a low-priority concern and that arrests of offenders are purposely avoided. There are several reasons why police agencies handle spouse abuse the way they do. Family or domestic violence has traditionally been regarded as a private matter. Many police officers resent becoming involved in spouse abuse because it takes so much time away from their major duties of crime fighting in the streets. One consideration is the amount of time involved in processing a case of this nature. Often, the wife reports abuse several times in a row, then decides against pressing charges and returns home only to call the police the next day with the same complaint. This costs the taxpayers millions in dollars and diverts police personnel from responding to other emergencies.

Until recently, many state and local statutes prohibited an officer from making an arrest without witnessing the abuse. Almost half of our states now have laws that give police the authority to make an arrest on probable cause, which does not require a warrant.

Spouse abuse, to most, is defined as physical abuse or violent acts suffered between spouses, both male and female. Very few men, however, file complaints with the local police stating that their wives are abusing them because their pride is at stake.

Spouse-beating may range from a simple slap or push to an injury requiring hospitalization, or to a serious incident involving the use of weapons. A simple argument can turn into a boxing match. It's quite common for a family to experience an argument that could be termed violent. It is also possible for one spouse on a rare occasion to accidentally lose control and hurt another during a heated argument. But when the rare one-time incident turns into a regularly-scheduled event, it's time to get help.

As with child abuse, spouse abuse is found at all levels of society.

In many cases, the victim taunts the offender until tempers flare. Comments like, "Why are you such a failure?", or, "I should have married someone else" can lead to an all-out argument, or to violence. Some family members even expect to be hit once in a while. Remarks like, "If he didn't hit me once in a while, I would think he didn't care anymore," are signs of deeper trouble.

Reported incidents of abuse indicate that abuse by men, as would be expected because of their size and strength, is more apt to result in serious injury. But when a woman decides to fight back, she is more likely to acquire a weapon, such as a knife or gun, to assist her.

What Can Be Done?

Unlike the victim of child abuse, the spouse suffering the abuse can, in most cases, pack up and leave, although many women lack the emotional or financial resources to do so. Legal recourse is an option, and separation or divorce often follow. But if both parties agree, professional marriage counseling may save the marriage. Talking with family members or a close friend can possibly alleviate the problems related to the abuse. Similar family pressures and stress situations are present in both spouse abuse and child abuse cases. Just as most child abuse situations can be resolved, most spouse abuse can end if both spouses are willing to make the necessary efforts.

Where To Get Help

- Local public services for support and counseling to battered wives. These agencies can be located in your telephone directory under such headings as "Battered Women," and "Domestic Violence." Call them for help and advice.
- Local police and hospitals.

The total number of injuries resulting from child abuse and spouse abuse is staggering. For many victims, the dangers at home are far greater than those on the street. But at least when the threat of abuse is recognized, it can be cornered and eliminated, unlike many social crimes that exist outside the family. Many tormented families can, with help, learn to cope with their problems without resorting to violence.

CHAPTER THIRTEEN

The Law and Self Defense

Chris Martin is finding it hard to believe that his so-called actions of self defense will probably land him behind bars for several years, charged with manslaughter. After a dispute erupted over a pool game, Peter Turri attacked Martin who was able to overtake Turri and gain control. However, according to witnesses, once Martin was in control, he continued to beat the other man into unconsciousness. Turri later died of internal bleeding.

Who is the Victim?

> "A skillful warrior strikes a decisive blow and stops. He does not continue his attack to assert his mastery. He will strike the blow, but be on his guard against being vain or arrogant over his success. He strikes it as a matter of necessity, but not from a wish of mastery."
>
> — *Lao Tzu*

Everyone has the legal right to defend themselves against acts of violence and aggression. However, you must understand the law regarding reasonable and necessary force to make sure you do not end up facing prosecution.

If you were to be found guilty of unnecessary force, resulting in an assault charge, you might find yourself not only a defendant in a criminal charge, but a defendant in a civil charge. The criminal charge is based on legal (public) wrongdoing, which affects the public. If convicted of a criminal charge, the defendant may be fined and/or imprisoned, as ordered by the court. Legal wrongs can be either civil or criminal wrongs.

The civil charge (commonly known as a tort) is a civil (private) wrongdoing, which affects a person or his property. If convicted of a civil charge (found liable), the defendant may be ordered to pay compensatory and punitive damages to the victim(s).

Thus a single deed could result in two prosecutions. The circumstances, as in all cases, and the injuries suffered, play major roles in whether the judge and jury determine that sufficient cause was present to warrant a forcible defense.

What is Reasonable and Necessary Force?

Reasonable is defined as "not excessive or extreme." Necessary is defined as, "needed to achieve a certain result; essential." By definition, then, reasonable and necessary force is that which would not be considered excessive or extreme, but essential and needed to achieve a certain result.

Pay close attention to this definition. Many people interpret this law in different ways. Depending on which side of the jailer's bars you sit, the interpretation can be critical. Each state has its own definition of self-defense and reasonable force. A consistent definition does not currently prevail throughout the United States. To learn how your state defines self-defense and necessary force, contact your county prosecutor for a precise interpretation.

As a general rule, most prosecutors agree that reasonable and necessary force is that used to resist what is believed to be an immediate and imminent danger, and the defendant must also believe that the use of such force is necessary to avoid injury or death. In other words the defendant had NO alternative. In terms of this definition, we can assume that the intent of the aggressor is to cause immediate and imminent danger. I emphasize that this is not your intent but that of the aggressor. Justifying the use of self-defense and having it stand up in court depends on who is being attacked. You cannot be the initial aggressor and expect to use the self-defense plea effectively in court. Let's look at some examples.

Bill walks up to order a drink at a bar and intentionally shoves and pushes his way past Mike, who has been patiently waiting in line to order. Now Mike shoves back and Bill punches Mike in the mouth.

Bill could be charged with and found guilty of assault and battery, because he was the initial aggressor. But Mike was technically wrong to shove back since there was no immediate or imminent threat of physical violence. For all Mike knew, Bill could have accidentally stumbled into him. This can become a bit confusing, but it is important to look at the overall picture and consider what the legal ramifications could be.

When you consider the long-range consequences, it can be better to overlook a small incident than to have it turn out to be big headache. It really is better to walk away or talk your way out of any confrontation, wherever possible. Simply avoid it!

But there are several other factors involved here—let's look at Bill and Mike again. In the situation just described, Bill was considered the initial aggressor. If, however, after being shoved back by Mike, Bill attempted to flee the area and Mike jumped on his back and wrestled Bill to the ground, Bill would now be legally justified in defending himself.

Now, in another situation, Bill threatens Mike verbally and begins to pull back his fist, obviously preparing to punch. Mike does not have to wait to receive the actual punch before applying force in defense. This threat would be considered immediate and real. If, for some reason, Bill were standing across the room and made the same threat, Mike would not be justified in using force because there was no element of immediate danger.

Use of Force to Defend Another

The same rationale for defending oneself applies when defending another. The same principles exist.

If you feel that a person is in immediate and imminent danger, and they can neither avoid nor defend against the situation, you are justified in using reasonable and necessary force to counter the threat. There is no law that requires you to come to the aid of someone being threatened or assaulted, nor is there ever likely to be one. The decision is strictly yours. In some situations, by interfering with an act of violence you may place the victim in even greater danger.

From a different viewpoint, consider what could happen if you should decide to come to the defense of a person being assaulted, and during the ensuing struggle with the criminal the victim is accidentally injured or killed. If the victim survives, you could be sued for damages because your actions possibly resulted in his injury. Or the surviving family may sue you for causing the victim's death. Needless to say, there are many things to consider before you become involved in situations of this nature. Usually, a person does what he feels is morally and legally right and expects a fair decision in return.

Use of Deadly Force

Another very important principle which also must be understood is the use of deadly force, which is generally defined as the force used to prevent immediate and imminent death or great bodily harm. To be justified in using deadly force (it would be wise to consult your prosecutor's office for a precise reading here also), the basic elements are as follows:

First, if a person can escape without risking danger he, in many jurisdictions, is required to do so. However, in other jurisdictions, you have the right to stand and fight, especially if you take your stand on your property or in your home. Common sense should be followed in all situations. Even though you may legally stand your ground and defend to the death, it might make more sense to run away and avoid an unnecessary danger if possible. This same principle applies when in defense of another.

Deadly force should never be intentionally used:

- Against non-deadly force.
- When alternate defenses can be used.
- Based on suspicion of activity alone.
- Against a person attempting to flee.
- Against a person damaging or threatening to damage property.

Defending Property

The use of force or the threat of force to protect one's property is generally acknowledged as a proper defense when a person believes that his property is being illegally threatened. However, such force may only be used as a last resort if assistance from law enforcement officers is not immediately available and reasonable attempts to verbally stop the aggressor fail. Again, only the force that is necessary to stop the intruder can be applied, and no more.

When You May Use a Weapon

A weapon can be any object that when used offensively or defensively assists the user in accomplishing his goals. We know when we are justified in using deadly force. Are we authorized, however, to gain the advantage with the use of a weapon? If the aggressor has a weapon to aid him, then, as a general rule, we may employ our own weapon with as much force as necessary to defend ourselves. Remember, you have the right to use deadly force when you feel immediate, imminent threat of death or bodily harm.

"Booby Traps" to Protect Property

Many different opinions and court decisions have been handed down on the use of the devices, commonly called "booby traps," used to deter intruders. Most states advise that the value of human life outweighs that of property. The general reason for employing such devices is to keep intruders from entering an established property or dwelling—by the threat of, or use of deadly force—when the owner or occupant is not around to do so personally. Here, then, the courts contend that there was no immediate and imminent threat to the owner, invalidating the use of deadly force. The possibility of an innocent person becoming a victim of a well-placed "booby trap" is a likelihood that must be considered.

Different Definitions in Different Areas

Because of the variances in state statutes and court decisions across the country, readers are urged to consult with legal counselors and county prosecutors before assuming that these definitions are legally acceptable in their areas.

CHAPTER FOURTEEN

Weapons:
Are they Legal,
Safe, Effective?

Determined to prevent the burglar from breaking into the Elliott's home, 19-year-old babysitter Betsy Robbins grabbed a nearby golf club and repeatedly struck the would-be intruder on his arms and hands as he broke through the window. He lost his balance and fell back into the bushes below. Threatening to "beat his head in if he didn't leave," the dazed burglar managed to tumble off into the night, while Betsy called the police for help.

Her phone call did the trick—police picked up the disheartened criminal a half-mile out of town!

Are they Legal?

Whether you are for or against the use and possession of weapons, the knowledge of what constitutes a legal, safe, and effective weapon may be of benefit to you and your family.

NOTE: This book does not recommend that the reader employ the use of weapons as discussed herein. It only provides guidelines and sets examples of possible situations a person may be confronted with. Each person must search his own mind, soul and legal system to understand what is legal, safe and effective. Anytime a person faces a decision to defend himself, especially with the use of a weapon, he must choose what he feels is right at the moment to survive. However, once committed, the final responsibility as to what transpired lies with that individual.

Refer back to Chapter 13 concerning the law and use of force to refresh your memory as to when self defense is legally justified. It's important to always remember what is *reasonable* and *necessary* force.

According to the Second Amendment of the United States Constitution, every person in the United States has a constitutional right to possess firearms (excluding felons, minors, etc.). This does not mean that you may run out to your local gun shop, purchase a .44 magnum and strap it to your hip while doing your weekly shopping. Federal, state, and local laws regulate who may purchase firearms, and the type of firearms and ammunition legally available, including where and when they may be carried and discharged. Many other weapons, such as knives, clubs, and chemicals, are also regulated, but are legally available to authorized individuals.

Not everyone has an interest in firearms, let alone the desire or need to own one. There are many families who for personal or religious reasons never intend to obtain a weapon of any form. Many feel that for them, the mere presence of a weapon in their home constitutes an even greater threat than that of an intruder. This is very true. For those not safely trained in their use, or in families with many curious young children, a weapon may prove fatal. Even when safety is practiced, accidents happen.

To the individual raised in a home where firearms are used on a frequent basis, such as in hunting or target shooting, a weapon may be as familiar a piece of equipment as the family car. Both, of course, should be well respected.

Whatever position you take concerning weapons, pro or con, always be certain that your decision is intelligently made. Never forget to use common sense.

Be sure that:

- You obtain all weapons legally.
- All firearms and most other weapons have a serial number recorded on them.
- When purchasing a weapon, always obtain a bill of sale and register it with your local police department. (This allows it to be returned to the proper owner if stolen and recovered.)

- When in doubt about the weapon or its seller, report them to your local police.
- You understand the law in your area concerning weapons.
- You learn and practice safety with all weapons.
- You always store weapons in a safe place and use safety features such as trigger guards, locked cabinets, etc.
- Your weapon meets legal specifications.
- You attend updated safety courses on your weapon, and make certain that all individuals who are to handle the weapon can do so safely.
- You never play games with weapons. They are not toys.
- You never point a firearm (even if it is empty) at another person.

If you have specific questions about the possession and use of weapons, contact your local police department or prosecutor for assistance.

Are They Safe?

Most weapons have one thing in common: the ability to kill. If improperly or unsafely used, the owner or another innocent person may wind up an unintended victim. Accidents will happen, but they can be limited if people take the time necessary to learn and practice safety procedures. Safety must always be the number-one priority. "I didn't know the gun was loaded" is not a satisfactory excuse for accidentally shooting your wife, son, or daughter. Rules must be established and strictly enforced. In a home where firearms are located, all responsible family members should be taught the safeguards and procedures of firearms, and all members taught to respect the firearm. It is just a tool. It doesn't kill, the person holding it does. Always remember: if you abuse a firearm, or the rules of safety, someone could end up dead. You rarely get a second chance.

Are They Effective?

If you find it necessary to buy and use a weapon, don't take chances or risk its failure by getting the cheapest one available. Make sure that whatever you use, whether it's a shotgun or a butter knife, it is functional. Before you buy, examine several to find the one best suited to your needs. Test it for its effectiveness, and obtain the opinions of several knowledgable individuals before buying. Ask yourself, "Is this what I really need?" "Will it work effectively?,"

"Can I effectively use it?," and "What advantages and disadvantages does it have?" Once you are satisfied that you have chosen the weapon that is right for you, get the training needed to use it effectively and practice with it so that you can continue to do so. Take the necessary care of your weapon to keep it fully functional at all times.

Alternative Weapons

Not all weapons have to be specifically designed as such to be used as effective tools for defense. The **kitchen knife** is one tool that is found in every home. When necessary, this object can be used to defend against a would-be assailant. The **skillet,** or **frying pan,** can be quickly and effectively turned against an intruder. **Car keys** held tightly in your hand can painfully injure an attacker attempting to wrestle you to the ground. A **comb, pen,** or **pencil** can be jabbed into the eyes, throat, or groin of a rapist, providing sufficient time for an escape. **Hair spray** or **spray perfume** can temporarily blind an assailant. Your **cane** or **umbrella** can be used to defend against an attacker on the street or on the bus. (Chapter 15 provides more on these weapons.) These and other accessible objects can be quickly and effectively used to deter or defend against an attacker, although they were originally designed for other tasks.

Think ahead, and plan for emergencies. A weapon, when used, is simply an extension of one's arm. Understand and master your body first, then carry this attitude further with the use of weapons. Take the time to study your home or purse and determine what objects are within reach that could be employed during a surprise assault.

Firearms

Shotgun

The safest and most effective firearm available—by far—is the shotgun. It not only provides a visible psychological advantage, but when discharged, does not require perfect accuracy to be effective. A rifle or pistol fires a single bullet, but a single shot from a shotgun can release many pellets, which spread out, increasing the chances of hitting the target. A shoulder-fired weapon provides the user with a better sense of accuracy because the eye sights the target down the barrel, while the stock is supported against the shoulder and the barrel supported with the forward hand. The user can learn to line up the sights with the target with very little practice and discipline. A pistol, by constrast, is generally unsupported, and sighting is more difficult, requiring more time to effectively hit what you are aiming at.

But can a slightly built woman fire a shotgun effectively? Yes. the size of the user makes no difference, assuming we are not including small children.

Every person who uses a firearm should be certain that it is in good operating condition. Clean it regularly and thoroughly, and always check the barrels to make sure that no unwanted items have been placed inside. Install a rubber recoil pad on the butt of the stock. This pad is designed to reduce the recoil of the gun when fired, and can mean the difference between receiving a small push or a powerful kick and a bruise. The proper grip, and firm pressure against the shoulder, must always be used. Many people believe that the smaller the gun the smaller the kick, but the opposite is true—the bigger and heavier the gun, the less recoil experienced. Even though the operation of a shotgun can be learned quickly, it must be fired regularly to be sure the user remains effective.

There are many different calibers of shotguns to choose from. The most recommended are the 20, 16, and 12-gauges. The 12-gauge has the largest bore diameter. Many professionals would choose this as the best of the three, but any one of them will effectively serve your purpose.

Look for a shotgun with the shortest barrel legally available. This allows for a greater spread pattern of the shot fired and for increased mobility while moving from room to room searching for an intruder. Federal law prohibits the possession of a shotgun with a barrel length of 18 inches or less. Anything shorter would be considered a sawed-off shotgun, which is commonly used by criminals. Do not attempt to modify an existing shotgun barrel to 18 inches by simply sawing it off. That's a job for an experienced gunsmith.

Most shotguns on the market will be of single, pump, or double design. The single barrel can provide the firepower needed in most situations, especially if it's of the pump design. A single shot firearm requires reloading after each round fired, whereas a pump can provide as many as five rounds by "pumping," without removing the shotgun from your shoulder. By pumping or working the slide action, another round is chambered. The double-barrel is perhaps the easiest to operate. It's designed to break open, ejecting spent shells and, in most cases, one action automatically places the weapon on safety and cocks the weapon for the next round. All that is required is to simply reload two more shells, one into each barrel, and close the barrels back into position. Now, in order to fire, the user simply turns off the safety, then either pulls one trigger, or pulls both triggers at the same time.

Choosing the right shotgun should be done with careful planning. Ask a qualified salesman. As soon as you buy it, make arrangements for thorough instruction in its use, care, and safety. Scout around for a firearms training course near you, and see to it that everyone who anticipates using the firearm attends.

Some people prefer to keep their firearms loaded. Others, for safety reasons, keep their weapons empty, with ammunition nearby. It's up to you to determine which way is best after becoming thoroughly knowledgeable about your weapon and its individual characteristics.

Rifles

Rifles come in all calibers and sizes. For the most part, a rifle requires more training, practice, and maintenance than the shotgun. Accuracy is very important, and because only one bullet is fired at any one time, considerable practice is necessary to learn to use it effectively and to develop individual confidence in its use.

A major hazard of a rifle is that when it is fired, the round can travel great distances—through walls—thereby endangering others, possibly someone sleeping in the next room. For outdoor use, such as on a ranch a rifle is fine. If you own a rifle and do not plan to buy a shotgun, obtain low-velocity bullets that have little power. They will still stop an intruder, but will not usually travel through solid objects. As with the shotgun, the ideal home-defense rifle should have a short barrel for maneuverability.

Whatever rifle you choose, use round-nosed ammunition, which is made of soft lead. This bullet will not penetrate or ricochet to the extent that other ammunition does. For home-defense purposes, buy a shotgun, if possible. If you already own a rifle, make sure you are totally familiar with it and can use it effectively in an emergency. Seek out an expert in your area and learn all there is to know, both good and bad, about using a rifle for home defense.

Handguns

The handgun is a very effective weapon, and is easily concealed. In street situations, the pistol is the only weapon that can offer both concealment and firepower. In a home, its concealment makes it more difficult to locate, and it can be difficult to fire and hit your target unless you have remained proficient by constant practice. As a last resort, though, a handgun can prove very effective.

Professionals recommend the revolver—.38, .357, or automatic .45 caliber—for defensive shooting. The .38 is the best in most home situations. Most pistols of this type are very simple to use. They have a five- or six-shot capacity, allowing the cylinder to open quickly for reloading.

Many prefer to load a six-shot pistol with five rounds, leaving one cylinder empty. This way, if the gun is taken away from and turned on you, you would know that you had one click of the trigger during which to react. Be careful that you know which way your cylinder turns when doing this. Some, like the Smith & Wesson .38, rotate counterclockwise, while others, such as the Colt, rotate clockwise.

Barrel length can vary from two to six inches for standard pistols. Four- or six-inch barrels are the most recommended models for the home. Two-inch barrels are mainly used for plain-clothes police, or security people, who need concealment and firepower at close range.

Generally, most pistols can be fired in two different ways. First, simply pulling the trigger operates the hammer, which fires the round and rotates the cylinder to the next round. This is called double-action and requires more trigger pressure than single-action, but provides rapid fire. In a single-action pistol, the hammer is intentionally pulled back, cocking the weapon before pulling the trigger. It takes very little pressure to pull the trigger, but the action is slower because of the time required to cock and pull.

Although most revolvers have no additional safety features, most modern models are designed to prevent the gun from firing if dropped. Even if your weapon has this feature, avoid dropping it.

The automatics (which are actually semi-automatic) on the market, such as the .45 and 9mm, are very effective in police work in terms of stopping-power, but most automatic ammunition penetrates and travels a considerable distance before stopping. They are generally more difficult to handle and fire, but they hold up to fifteen rounds for greater firepower. They are harder to service and require more practice to achieve and maintain accuracy.

Automatics usually offer more safety features than revolvers, but this can be a hindrance in an emergency if the operator is not aware of these features.

As with all firearms, understanding the weapon's unique characteristics and practicing regularly are required to insure its effective use as a means of defense. Proper instruction is vital, as is maintaining proficiency in their use. Always practice *safety* and never play games with a weapon.

Practice

Once you understand exactly what your firearm does and how it works, you must practice, as needed, to remain proficient.

Always practice the loading, cocking, and firing process until you can do it blindfolded; never, however, attempt it blindfolded, for this is unsafe! Do practice at least the first two phases in the dark, and locate a firing range that will let you shoot safely in a dark environment to familiarize you with what it would be like at home at night.

Dry-fire your gun with an empty shell casing in the cylinder for trigger-pull practice.

When obtaining instruction in defensive shooting, remember that you should be concerned with aiming for the center of mass of the target and not the bullseye. When facing a threatening situation, you probably won't have time to take careful aim before firing. Emphasis must be placed on first concealing yourself, then quickly aiming for the center of the assailant's body to insure a hit on the first round. You might not have either the time or the opportunity for a second. If you can afford the time, however, always take careful aim.

Once back home, make sure that your weapon is empty and placed in its secure location. Now, practice a few dry runs—imagine that someone is breaking down your door. How long does it take to reach it? Is the ammunition handy? Can you secure the door for protection?

To remain proficient in anything, a person must continue to practice. Keep this in mind.

Securing the Firearm

Buying a firearm is one thing. Securing it is another. When a wife and husband are the only two people residing in their house, securing a weapon is relatively easy and safe. When a family has children who are not old enough to understand the potential dangers associated with firearms, properly securing the firearm is of prime importance.

Since you probably own a firearm for protection, the ability to locate it and load it quickly during an emergency is, of course, important. How can you accomplish this and still insure adequate safety for your children? Additionally, how can you secure any weapon to guard against a possible burglar stealing it? Consider these guidelines:

- Register all weapons with your local police department.
- Lock all weapons in a lockable drawer or container, if possible. Keep the key controlled and accessible.
- Install a burglar-resistant firearms cabinet.
- Secure the weapon on a high shelf or a lockable closet.
- Apply trigger locks, which prevent the use of a firearm.
- Open the revolver cylinder and attach a padlock through the top of the frame, preventing operation.
- If you store a firearm in a dresser drawer next to the bed, always keep it unlocked. Use a speed loader device for revolvers, and a loaded clip for automatics. This procedure is safe and will allow you time to load in case of an emergency.
- Keep ammunition locked up during the day or in another location. At night, when you feel you need the safety of your firearm, place the ammunition inside the drawer with your weapon.

Firearm Safety:

- Thoroughly understand the characteristics of each weapon.
- Always *assume* your weapon is loaded.
- Always double-check a weapon to see if it is loaded; never take another person's word. (This is not disrespect, but just

a good common-sense safety measure.)

- Never point any weapon at another living object unless you intend to shoot it.
- When under the influence of alcohol or medication, keep away from all weapons to prevent accidents.
- Never allow children to *play* with a weapon. (They may sneak into your room, remove the weapon and play games with it.)
- Always empty, then dry-fire (pull the trigger) your firearm prior to storing or transporting it.
- Always check the barrel for unauthorized objects that may have fallen into it.
- Always protect your weapon from damage.
- Clean and oil your weapon regularly.
- Never fire old, questionable ammunition from a firearm.
- Always secure weapons properly.
- When firing a weapon, always be sure the target area is safe and that there is no possibility for a round to travel or ricochet in the direction of another living thing.
- Wear ear protection when firing a weapon.
- Always keep the barrel of a weapon pointing down-range.
- Never hand a weapon to another person with your finger on the trigger. Open the cylinder of a revolver or lock the slide of an automatic back prior to handing it to him.
- Practice emergency procedures that test the ability to obtain, load, and conceal oneself for defense against an intruder. However, always practice with your family's safety in mind. Remember, this is not a game and should never be treated as such.

Using a Club

As an instrument to strike with, a club can be a forceful, effective means of defense. Strategically placed throughout the home, police batons, baseball bats, and golf clubs can all be used to attack or defend against an intruder.

When swinging a club, always grasp it firmly with both hands, applying the force you think you need to disable an assailant. Never continue beating even a criminal once he is either unconscious or totally disabled. You could be charged with assault. Remember, use only the force necessary to defend yourself.

When the assailant is using a weapon, try to strike his hands and arms, then follow up with strikes to the legs and feet, in order to overpower him. Try not to strike him in the head because this may prove fatal.

Using a Knife

Among all the possible weapons available throughout the world, the knife is unmatched in terms of usefulness. It is used as a tool, as well as a form of defense, and is found in one form or another in every home.

The art of knife-fighting, like all forms of defense, requires many years of proper instruction and practice to acquire discipline and skill, and to develop the proper attitude. The average person does not need to be a combat-effective knife-fighter. If you understand the basic concepts involved in knife defense, and if you practice simple techniques, you should be able to apply basic, effective defensive or offensive techniques when they are required.

In nearly every home in the world, a knife can be found in the kitchen, the garage, or the barn. Knives offer a unique form of defense and can quickly be secured for protection, especially when needed for close, hand-to-hand contact. A small person wielding a knife can face a much larger aggressor and even the odds dramatically.

Knives are available in a variety of sizes, shapes, and designs to perform specific tasks. The hunter's knife must withstand the rugged outdoors, be razor-sharp and flexible enough to skin game. The commando's combat knife is double-edged, razor-sharp, and fairly heavy. Its double edge provides a clean double cut-slice insertion, while preventing the assailant from grabbing the blade and attempting to twist it free during a struggle. The typical kitchen knife is not necessarily razor-sharp and often has a round point. However, with enough power behind it in attacking a vital area, this knife can prove very effective.

Principles of Knife Defense/Offense

When escape is impossible and you find yourself facing an advancing criminal who has forced his way into your home, defensive and offensive measures may be necessary. If you have warned an intruder to stop and he doesn't, and you fear bodily harm or death, you have a right to defend yourself, using whatever force is necessary.

If armed with nothing more than a knife, you must understand basic characteristics of knife defense and offense. Always face your assailant and attempt to discern his intentions. If you are able to frighten him off, do so. Avoid any contact, if possible, but if he continues, you must stop him before you become his next victim.

1. Secure the knife with a tight grip in your strong hand.
2. Keep away from the assailant, then attempt to escape or defensively ward off his attack.
3. Once the assailant lunges at you, take whatever actions are necessary to stop him.
4. If you decide to employ offensive tactics, be sure to concentrate your attack on a vital point. (Figure 14-1.)
5. Once you attack, follow through completely, using power to insure an effective attack.
6. Simple flesh wounds may or may not incapacitate or scare off an assailant. However, simple injuries inflicted on a desperate criminal may cause him to turn and fight when he might otherwise have fled.
7. After you have gained control over an attacking criminal, notify the police and medical services immediately.

Figure 14-1 **Knife Vital Striking Points**

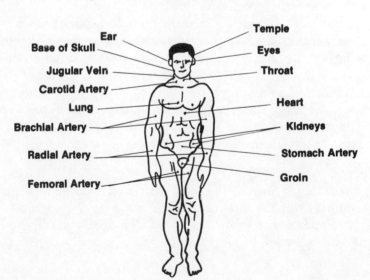

Holding the Knife

There are two basic methods for holding a knife for defense. The palm grasp, similar to that of a fencer grasping his sword, is used primarily for slashing and jabbing *(Figure 14-2.)* It is used to keep an aggressor at a distance and is considered an outside fighting technique. Injuries inflicted by this method are rarely fatal unless the strike is deep and penetrates a vital organ. Disadvantages of this grip are that it can be trapped, deflected, or kicked out of the fighter's hand.

Figure 14-2

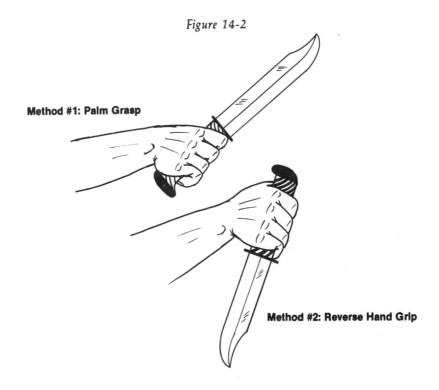

Method #1: Palm Grasp

Method #2: Reverse Hand Grip

The reverse hand grip is used for hiding the knife prior to attack and provides the maximum killing power when striking. This technique is used to confuse or surprise an attacker while getting close and inside, then spinning and exploding with a powerful reverse hand strike, burying it deep into a vital area. The victim will usually suffer a great loss of blood, lapse into unconsciousness, and die if medical attention is not given immediately.

- Any weapon can be turned against its user.
- Knife wounds are not always fatal and do not always incapacitate a person.
- If used unnecessarily against an innocent person, criminal and civil charges can be brought against you. Even if used against an intruder, you may still be held liable for your actions.

When Facing a Knife-Wielding Assailant

- Always attempt to run away.
- Use *any* weapon to defend against the attacker.
- Wrap your belt, shirt, or jacket around your hand, wrist, and arm to defend against the attacker.
- Use a chair to keep an attacker away.
- Apply knife defenses as discussed in Chapter 15.

The only way to become proficient with a knife is to practice. It is not necessary to actually hold a knife in your hand to do this. Work with a partner, switching the roles of aggressor and victim, and simulate an actual incident that includes all possible actions.

Using a knife for defense is not easy and can be ugly. But the night you are left alone with a prowler trying to force his way inside your home, the company of your potato-peeler can feel pretty good. As a last resort, this little piece of steel can save your life from a crazy attacker or rapist.

Tear Gas and Mace

Chemical tear gas and mace are available almost anywhere, and can provide an effective, temporary means of defense when used properly. The secret of its use is to spray it at the chest or throat of an assailant so that it forms a gaseous cloud which affects the eyes. Spraying it directly into the eyes will usually prove ineffective. The biggest problems associated with mace or tear gas are that:

- The user never practices with it. (It may dry up or never work to begin with.)
- It's attached to a key chain or buried in the bottom of a purse and the owner eventually forgets she even has it.

- It is sometimes difficult to get to, when it's needed, and pointing it in the right direction may be a problem.
- Children may stumble upon it on a key chain or in a purse and accidentally discharge it.

Like any other weapon, it must be thoroughly understood and mastered. Practice to learn its effectiveness. Once you are proficient in its use, be prepared to use it at any time.

CHAPTER FIFTEEN

Defensive Techniques

When All Else Fails

This chapter was written with the reader's safety in mind. It neither stresses nor recommends that a person employ defensive or offensive measures when other options are available. Defensive tactics should be used only as a last resort. However, for reasons only you can determine, there may come a time when you must stand, defend, and/or fight to survive.

Many incidents can be settled safely with a simple apology or by just walking away. A wild two-minute struggle could leave you or another person injured or crippled for life. How would your family survive if you were disabled and they were dependent upon you for support? Nobody ever wins by becoming involved in foolish acts that serve no legitimate purpose. Defense is strictly a means to stop or control aggression.

When studying defense, we must look closely at offense, for where there is one, you always find the other. Our goal, when attacked, should be to defend, then escape unharmed. To stick around and play "Captain America" could get you killed. Escape with the least amount of physical contact possible. If, however, the assailant continues a relentless attack, you may be forced to turn and strike back offensively, using whatever force is necessary to stop him. The name of the game quickly changes from defense to offense. Your attitude must also change. Survival is everything when someone tries to take life from you. It becomes the most basic of decisions: kill or be killed. When you find yourself facing your charging attacker, remain calm and think clearly. Relax, if possible, and call on all of your abilities to gain an advantage in the situation. Use the element of surprise to aid you in your attack. All offensive techniques on your part must be applied forcefully, at just the right time, and targeted at the attacker's weakest point. When you remain calm, your awareness becomes keen and your reactions sharp. Watch and wait for an opening in your opponent's defense. This may come when he glances away, tries to regain his breath and balance, drops his guard, or switches a weapon from one hand to another. When you unleash your attack, move swiftly and confidently, and above all, do not cease your attack until your adversary is down for the count! This sounds drastic, but it's absolutely necessary when your life hangs in the balance.

With these thoughts in mind, study the following techniques and become proficient in their use. Once you can adequately apply these techniques, practice them in different environments, such as in a dark, small room, or in a hallway. Combine several techniques and incorporate them into a practice session you can work on with a partner. Plan realistic scenarios and work out the best defensive—as well as offensive—tactics for you. Ask yourself, "Will this work effectively against a large person, a small person, a man, or a woman?"

Before you can learn to be an effective offensive fighter, you must first become well-versed and skilled in defensive techniques. You can be the best boxer with the quickest hands in town, but if you cannot prevent your opponent from striking you first, you may never get the opportunity to strike back. Using this philosophy, study the following photographs closely; observe the step-by-step instructions. When you understand them, practice each step individually. Then combine them until you can easily apply the entire process smoothly, fluidly, and with good coordination. If you are alone, visualize an imaginary aggressor attacking you, then apply your technique, making sure that you follow through each step completely. When possible, work with a partner who can physically apply "controlled aggression," allowing you to perform each technique and at the same time provide a little "safe" resistance.

No book can substitute for the "real thing" as effectively as classroom instruction and training by a qualified instructor. But the written word, when combined with illustrations, can be an effective guide to the tried-and-true techniques that are likely to work best for the individual who is serious about self-defense.

Never limit yourself in training. Learn to adapt to as many situations as possible. Use what works and throw away techniques that hinder your abilities. Study as much as possible to increase your capacity to make the most intelligent decisions in the least amount of time. Every person has weaknesses and strengths. The techniques that follow will work on 99 percent of the aggressors you are ever likely to confront. (There is always that one percent that will give you difficulty.) If you are a one-hundred-pound male or female, you can effectively defend against a two-hundred-and-fifty-pound person if:

1. You know how and where to block or strike and run.
2. You practice combinations of techniques to make them instinctive. If one technique does not work, switch to another.
3. You defend or attack quickly, with every bit of effort available, and follow through completely.
4. You understand that you can survive and develop confidence in your training, thereby developing a new degree of confidence in yourself. Attitude is critical.

Search for all of the strong, effective techniques you can apply and capitalize on them. At the same time, find weaknesses in your adversary and capitalize on them, exploiting them to your advantage.

The following techniques are shown individually, in sequence, to enable you to follow each move slowly, one step at a time. Don't think in terms of the victim's vulnerability to counter-moves by the assailant. Understand that to learn a technique properly, you must first learn one move at a time. Once mastered, the moves join together to form a technique. These techniques should be practiced in different combinations, along with their counter-moves.

Seven Components of Good Defense/Offense

1. **Balance**—Maintain yours and keep your opponent off his. No technique, defensive or offensive, can be properly applied without correct balance.
   - Bend slightly at the knees.
   - Feet should be shoulder-width apart at any angle.
   - Weight should be evenly distributed between the legs and over the hips.

- Keep your back straight, head up, and stay alert.
- Shift your weight accordingly, keeping the center of gravity over your hips. (Balance in motion.)
- Never overextend.

2. **Leverage**—Use muscles properly to overcome your opponent. Take advantage of your strength when opportunity permits. However, never try to out-muscle your opponent. Out-think him. By combining proper muscle leverage with good balance and timing, you can out-maneuver the aggressor.

3. **Proper Techniques**—Combine defensive and offensive techniques. Knowing when and how to react while automatically applying effective techniques, is essential to gain control or overpower an aggressor.

4. **Utilization of Aggressor's Power**—Go with the flow. Always take advantage of your aggressor's momentum. Push when you are being pulled, and pull when you are being pushed. Through practice with a partner, you can develop the feel of "balance in motion," enabling you to take the necessary defensive or offensive measures while struggling. Concentration of power is critical the first time you attempt a technique. Attack the assailant's weakest point, using the maximum force you have developed through concentration.

5. **Timing**—It is very important to meet your opponent's attack at the proper time to take advantage of his momentum and to place you in a controlled position. You don't want your defense to arrive ahead of a punch. You want to stop short of it or slide past it, causing the aggressor to over-extend. This skill, too, improves with practice. To do this, you must understand components 1 through 4 thoroughly, practice diligently, and develop the ability to "feel" when it's right to move!

6. **Quick and Direct**—Do not hesitate between moves, and above all never perform techniques only halfway. Move with confidence. Pick your target and go for it. When your mind is sure, your body will be sure. Poor coordination and weak techniques are a result of the slow, indirect tactic.

7. **Follow Through**—Once you begin, follow through completely, applying techniques to their maximum potential. Commit yourself, or the end result could prove to be an ineffective application of your technique, and a waste of valuable energy and time. You might not get a second chance!

"Defensive" Attitudes of Avoid, Deflect, and Block

My philosophy in life, when faced with a problem, is to solve it the best way possible. In doing so, I choose the easiest and most effective solutions available. Why do it the hard way when I can take the path of least resistance? When faced with an oncoming problem, or in this case, "threat," I attempt to *avoid* it. If I cannot avoid it, then I try to *deflect* it. In other words, I make as little contact as necessary to overcome the obstacle and escape. But if I have no alternative other than to face it, I meet it head on in order to *block* it or stop it in its tracks. Obviously, it is preferable to avoid it altogether. If you understand this philosophy, carry it on through this chapter. It can help you in every possible threat situation, as well as throughout life.

Avoid

This is a *passive*, strictly defensive, maneuver, such as turning and walking away or taking another route to your destination. This includes sidestepping, bending, rolling, or jumping, literally out of the path of a punch or kick. This allows you to recover to an offensive posture if necessary, or to simply walk or run away.

Deflect

Deflection is a form of *soft defense*, where you meet the opposing force, glancing off of it, slipping by, redirecting or shifting balance through deflection of the opponent's power. This includes using deflecting blocks, and tripping techniques—the idea of "push and pull." It enables you to use very little of your own energy while forcing your aggressor to concentrate his, and to maintain control without having it become a "knock-down, drag-out fight." Properly applied, your assailant will lose his balance while you maintain yours. If necessary, you can follow up with a solid offensive technique to end the threat situation, or just keep deflecting until the aggressor quits out of frustration.

Block

The *hard defensive* maneuver is used when you are confronted with a direct threat which you cannot avoid or deflect. This is employing force against force. Your energy is being expended in an effort to counter or stop the aggressor quickly and effectively through forceful direct blocks, striking blocks, or forceful throws.

Finally, retreat—move back or out of a threat situation *in control*.

Vulnerability Points

Understand simple anatomy, know where to strike, if necessary, as well as where to avoid being hit. You can take advantage of certain vulnerability points that all humans have to assist you to temporarily incapacitate an aggressor. Review the anatomy chart and learn where a well-placed strike or kick will drop an attacker. (Figures 15-1 and 15-2.)

Figure 15-1

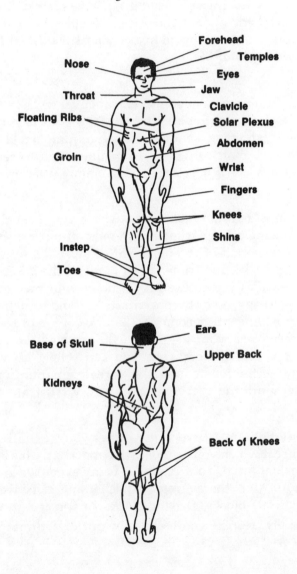

Figure 15-2

STRIKING POINTS

Target	Weapon	Action
Forehead	Punch/kick	Stunning effect/unconsciousness
*Temples	Punch/kick	Stunning effect/unconsciousness/death
*Eyes	Finger jab	Temporary blindness/unconsciousness/ pain/death
Nose	Punch/kick/knee-strike	Blood flow/watery eyes/much pain
Ears	Slap/punch	Much pain
Jaw	Punch/kick	Much pain
Base of skull	Punch/kick	Stunning effect/unconsciousness
*Throat	Punch/chop/kick	Loss of breath/death
Clavicle	Punch/kick	Bone break, loss of control of shoulder & arm
Upper back	Punch/kick/knee-strike	Much pain
Solar Plexus	Punch/elbow strike kick/knee strike	Loss of breath/unconsciousness
Floating ribs	Punch/kick/knee-strike	Loss of breath/bone-break/much pain
Abdomen	Punch/kick/knee-strike	Loss of breath
Wrist	Knuckle rap	Control maneuver/pain
Fingers	Pull/punch/bite	Control maneuver/pain
*Groin	Punch/kick/chop/ knee strike	Much pain/unconsciousness/death
Knees (front/side)	Kick	Break into collapse/much pain
Knees (back)	Kick	Collapse
Shins	Kick/punch	Much pain
Instep	Kick/punch	Much pain
Toes	Stomp/punch	Much pain

NOTE: Striking points marked with * indicate extremely *deadly* points. Use discretion when attacking these areas.

Training

Serious training is required to become proficient in applying defensive and offensive techniques. Study these training procedures to develop and maintain this proficiency. Remember: never undertake any potentially hazardous physical activity without first checking with your physician.

The Warm-Up

In most cases, controlled and limited practice will not require you to engage in a rigorous warm-up program, but it is generally recommended to warm up your body's systems prior to any practice that you know will strain your system. A basic warm-up will prepare your muscles, ligaments, and tendons for action and help prevent sprains, tears, and pulls. An injured muscle may require weeks or months to heal, so a few minutes of preparation makes good common sense. Warm-ups need not be physically exhausting, but the more active you are, the better you will develop physically.

Recommended Warm-Up Drill

1. First, start with running in place for about 60 seconds to shake out the knots and to get your blood flowing.
2. Next, do 25 jumping jacks at a moderate pace.
3. Get your wind, then do approximately 10 knee raises with each leg, gradually trying to touch your knees to your chest.
4. Now do 10 complete trunk rotations to the right. Stop. Then do 10 to the left.
5. Extend your arms straight out to your sides, and circle them forward, starting with small circles. Gradually make the circles larger and then smaller again for approximately 30 seconds. Stop. Now repeat the exercise, rotating your arms to the back.
6. Working your way upward, do neck twists to prevent neck muscle injury. Rotate your head to the left for approximately 10 seconds, then reverse for another 10 seconds.
7. Conclude the warm-up with another 25 jumping jacks.

This drill is not designed to completely prepare you for advanced workouts, such as high kicking, etc. Modify this program to meet your individual needs and desires. Try including leg stretching from the ground, and add other effective drills as necessary. For the purposes of this book, these drills will warm you up enough to conduct defensive training without injury.

Equipment

Contrary to popular belief, it is not necessary to purchase expensive training equipment to practice effectively. Many items that are found around the house can be turned into effective training aids for realistic training. If you intend to purchase, try to obtain equipment that will stand up to your practice sessions without falling apart.

Heavy Bag
Figure 15-3

Small Bag
Figure 15-4

Speed Bag
Figure 15-5

Top and Bottom Bag
Figure 15-6

Hanging Paper Target
Figure 15-7

The Heavy Bag

You have probably seen the heavy bag *(Figure 15-3)* inside your local gym or on television. One of the most effective training aids available, it is used to develop power in your punch and kick. Training can be conducted individually on the bag, taking advantage of its free-swinging action to develop footwork, timing, and the ability to judge distance in an attack. An excellent timing drill is performed by forcefully swinging the bag, then practicing ducking and punching at it as it swings. For resistance, another person can brace the bag, allowing you to fire away with full power while concentrating on technique. Continued training with the heavy bag develops the muscles in your arms, shoulders, legs, and back. When using this bag, as well as other striking bags, it is recommended that the practitioner wrap his hands before any workout. This is not so much to protect the skin as it is to protect the bones and muscles in the hands and wrists. This is usually accomplished by wrapping knuckles and wrists properly with tape (or even an ace bandage). The wrap should be snug but not so tight that it cuts off circulation. If you have difficulty with this, ask the boxing or karate instructor at the nearest YMCA or your local high school for assistance.

The heavy bag should be suspended on strong supports and have enough room to swing freely in all directions. Once you begin punching, always be sure your hands are clenched tightly prior to contact with the bag. All strikes should be forceful and well-directed. Concentrate on your techniques. Visualize the path of your strikes, and picture the end result of a successful punch. Also visualize an attack as you throw your punch or kick. After a while you will develop the ability to feel when each technique is done correctly, like a golfer or baseball player who knows his swing was perfect, connecting with the ball at the best possible time, sending it off into eternity. Sufficient training on this bag will develop endurance and stamina, both of which are desirable traits in your day-to-day environments.

The best way to understand what it feels like to hit another person is to strike a heavy bag. Here it is not necessary to pull your punches. The only other alternative is to actually strike another person. Stick with the bag for now; it rarely hits back.

Heavy bags can be purchased in a variety of weights and sizes. I recommend the 70-pound bag since it provides an excellent amount of resistance which closely resembles an actual adversary. An alternative to purchasing a new bag is to dig up an old military duffle bag and fill it with rags, foam, or carpet. It too provides a high degree of performance, and due to its rugged construction, will last a long time.

The Small Bag

The small bag *(Figure 15-4)* is not used by many students, mainly because there are other training devices more readily available. I have found though that it is probably the bag I rely on the most. It's portable, flexible, and can be easily raised and lowered by an ordinary piece of rope as training dictates. This bag allows the student to punch or kick it with full power, like the heavy bag, but unlike the heavy bag, provides little to no resistance. When struck, it collapses around the hand or foot, requiring a rapid withdraw to successfully set up for another combination. When punched correctly, it should collapse, but remain in one spot and not fly across the room. This develops hand and foot speed, which is necessary to correctly contact this bag, because if your hand moves too slowly, the momentum of the punch pushes the bag away. Your hand must move faster than the bag can react to keep it suspended in one spot. (This is what's happening if you have ever observed a martial artist breaking boards. His hand must strike and penetrate the board, breaking it before it can flex or fly away.) The nice thing about this bag is it can be made from scrap material at home very cheaply, or you can easily convert a laundry bag or pillowcase filled with old clothes into this very effective piece of equipment.

The Speed Bag

The speed bag *(Figure 15-5)* is another valuable tool in developing your defensive and offensive abilities. It is primarily used to develop, sharpen, and maintain hand speed and reactions. Mounted solidly on its platform, the speed bag should hang approximately at eye level. The student should stand approximately an arm's length from the bag. When striking this bag, the object is to develop a "rhythm in motion" action which helps both hand coordination and eye-hand coordination. Continued practice with this bag also develops the arms, shoulder, and back muscles. It is generally recommended to begin striking this bag with the front of the knuckles, switching to the back knuckles and/or side of the hand. But stick with one strike at a time until you catch on. Punch the bag twice with one hand and twice with the other. Develop the rhythm mentioned earlier. Eventually increase the number of strikes and types of strikes on each hand as you improve.

The Top and Bottom Bag

Quite different in appearance from the speed bag, the top and bottom bag is used to develop timing, improve reflexes and eye-hand coordination *(Figure 15-6)*. Suspended at shoulder level between two elastic ropes, this bag can be attacked from any angle. The object is to strike this bag squarely so that it comes directly back to the point of impact. Add a little footwork to the routine, dancing around the bag a little, and it becomes a formidable opponent. At first, you may find it difficult to master, but in time you should enjoy the many possible training techniques available through its use.

The Hanging Paper Target

Probably the quietest form of contact training that can be performed just about anywhere is done with the hanging paper target *(Figure 15-7)*. When the target is suspended by a piece of string tacked or taped to the ceiling, a person can practice all strikes and kicks with full power if desired. This very inexpensive piece of equipment provides an excellent form of speed training. You can strike at the target, stopping short, attempting to move it through the wind generated from a powerful strike or kick. Your ability to judge distance in your punches and kicks is greatly improved by the use of this simple training device, which sharpens the accuracy of each technique.

Used alone or all together, the training equipment we have discussed will greatly improve your overall defensive and offensive techniques. When working with them, don't view them simply as pieces of training equipment, but as real adversaries. Punch through them, not at them. Follow through on every technique, remembering the seven components of defense/offense. Make your training as realistic (but safe) as possible. Just because training equipment doesn't hit back is no reason to get lazy or overconfident.

Practice

Training alone is better than no training at all, but with the assistance of a training partner, practice is more realistic and more fun. Practice offensive and defensive techniques together, correcting each other along the way. Work on the techniques that give you difficulty until you feel confident of them. Always work with both hands and feet. Your weak side should be able to compensate for an injured strong arm or leg. Practice defending against more than one assailant.

Move your practice sessions outside. Try to obtain as much "live environment" training as possible. This means practice at night as well to understand how to face a real attack in the darkness. Develop your senses to perceive an attacker, even when he cannot be seen. Practice your technique in dark hallways and elevators, always keeping safety in mind, while attempting to keep your training as realistic as possible. There is nothing that says practice cannot be enjoyable. The more enjoyable and effective training is, the more a person practices. You are limited only by your imagination.

Balance

As discussed earlier, balance is one of the seven components of an effective defense/offense. The key is to maintain your balance at all times. Once you have perfected the ability to shift your weight evenly over your hips while moving—"balance in motion"—all techniques will be more effective. When training, always concentrate on proper balance, and never overextend yourself. Once you overextend, your balance is lost and so is any technique you are applying.

How can you develop balance? To start with, always keep it in mind. All day long, in every activity you become involved with, think balance. When dressing, expand the simple act of putting your socks and shoes on to improve balance. By raising your knee as high as possible (waist level is recommended) and holding your foot out in front of you for several seconds before putting on your socks and shoes, you learn to balance yourself in this position. It might take a while to learn to maintain your balance long enough to put your socks on, but eventually you will stop hopping around and bumping into everything.

Jumping rope is an excellent form of exercise, as well as a fine developer of balance. Try to jump rope on one foot for a while, then switch to the other while moving back and forth across the room. As you become more physically fit, you increase your ability to maintain balance in motion.

Coordination

Train with both hands and feet during each practice session. To develop your coordination and the ability to become ambidextrous, dress yourself with your weak hand regularly. Put your belt and tie on and brush your hair and teeth with your weak hand. At first it will be difficult, but eventually you can become proficient. These everyday activities will help improve your coordination, and strengthen your weak side.

A Final Word

During practice, always follow through with your intended technique. Never go only halfway because this develops bad habits that may lead to poorly executed techniques during an actual confrontation. Think positive. Practicing the techniques described in this chapter will help you develop a solid base from which to defend. Always seek additional training and instruction when possible. Be flexible and roll with the punches!

Basic Techniques

While studying and applying these basic techniques, remember to employ the seven components of defense/offense. If you are looking for advanced or flashy blocking, striking, or kicking techniques, you may be disappointed, but if you are interested in basic, effective techniques that do not require years of training to master, you will find the following pages interesting, practical, and very effective.

Basic Blocks

The key to a successful block is timing. Practice with a partner to increase your ability to judge distance, thereby improving your timing. When blocking, always attempt to do so with the minimum resistance, deflecting the oncoming punch or kick, if possible. Learn to effect each block with both arms to defend against an attacker at any angle.

There are three primary blocks that should be perfected. They are the *rising block*, the *crossing block*, and the *downward block*. Once these are mastered, you will be able to customize them to meet your needs and desires.

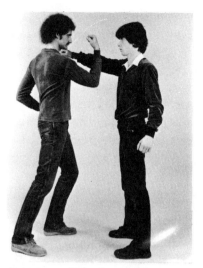

Rising Block: This is used to deflect or stop an attack that approaches from about shoulder level, and up.

Crossing Block: This one is used to deflect or stop an attack approaching at waist level, and up.

Downward Block: We use this to deflect or stop an attack approaching at waist level, and down.

Basic Strikes

As with blocking, timing is also very important when delivering a strike. A strike must also be initiated with enough force to affect its target. Throughout the following techniques, the punch, chop, finger jab; knuckle rap, elbow strike/smash, knee strike, and double hand slap will be utilized.

To increase the effectiveness of each strike, target it at the most vulnerable point of the aggressor.

Basic Kicks

Kicks are the most devastating of all offensive techniques, and require greater balance and accuracy than all other techniques to be effective. The kicks shown in this chapter are the side kick, stomp kick, shin kick, and groin kick. Even though a child with a basic understanding of self-defense can apply an effective kick, practice should be continued by everyone expecting to use them.

Combinations

Once you are able to apply the basic blocks, strikes, and kicks individually, you should learn to combine several of these techniques to form an arsenal of defensive and offensive maneuvers.

Stance

There are many different fighting styles, which utilize a variety of stances. Each person must find the stance that works for him whether he is attacking or defending. Every successful stance, however, has certain key elements.

A good stance is one that does not expose a large portion of the body to an attacker, and at the same time provides flexibility and balance. Body weight should be evenly distributed over your hips and supported equally by both legs. This allows for a quick advance or retreat, depending on what the situation calls for. Both hands should be held at approximately chest level with your elbows drawn close to your body for protection. Concentrate on using your lead hand for protection or blocking, as well as for quick strikes. The rear hand should be used primarily for power strikes, in addition to blocking.

Defending Against Weapons

Because of the risks involved in defending against an assailant, as I have pointed out, you should resist only as a last resort. Obviously, as the risks increase (an assailant is wielding a knife or gun), the need for submission may even be greater.

The basic techniques discussed here will work if learned and applied properly. More advanced techniques must be taught and supervised in a classroom environment by a competent instructor. However, since the knife is the most widely used weapon among criminals assaulting victims today, several different defensive techniques will be reviewed.

When facing an attacker who is holding a knife, it is most important to keep at a safe distance. Remove your coat or belt and wrap it around your defending arm or hand to absorb any strike. When you are grabbed and held by an attacker holding a knife to your throat, no defensive technique should be attempted until the opportunity for a safer defense presents itself. Obviously, the victim must determine if that opportunity will ever come, then act accordingly.

Defense Against Wrist Grab
(same arm) #1

Attacker (**A**) grabs victim's (**V**) wrist.

V immediately and with concentrated power snaps her wrist to palm-up position. This maneuver should break **A**'s grip.

V immediately strikes **A** in eyes with finger jab strike.

V supports herself on **A** while driving knee into **A**'s groin.

Defense Against Wrist Grab
(same arm) #2

Attacker (**A**) grabs victim's (**V**) wrist.

V immediately snaps her wrist to palm-up position.

V slaps her opposite hand under **A**'s hand and grasps it firmly.

See close ups.

V rotates her top hand over onto **A**'s hand sand wiching it between both hands then twists **A**'s wrist, sharply dropping **A** to his knees.

Defense Against Wrist Grab
(cross arm) #3

Attacker (**A**) grabs Victim's (**V**) opposite wrist.

V immediately snaps her wrist to palm-up position. This maneuver will force **A** to turn facing away from **V**.

V grabs **A**'s hand. She pulls back on **A**'s arm and side-kicks **A**'s near leg at side of knee, breaking knee cap.

A's leg collapses.

V then jerks **A**'s arm back and thrusts her knee into **A**'s back, then turns and runs to safety.

Defense Against
Arm Grab

Attacker (**A**) grabs victim's (**V**) arm with both hands.

V delivers finger jab strike to **A**'s eyes.

V completes technique with groin kick.

Defense Against Two Arm Shoulder Grab

Attacker (**A**) grabs victim's (**V**) shoulders.

V lowers her weight while cross-blocking (same arm) **A's** arm.

V then effects elbow strike to **A's** head.

Defense Against Bear Hug
(from front—over arms)

Attacker (**A**) grabs victim (**V**) in front bear hug over her arms.

V lowers her weight by slightly bending knees causing **A** to lean forward then grabs **A**'s hips.

V then executes groin strike with her knee.

V delivers elbow strike to **A**.

Defense Against Bear Hug
(from front—under arms)

Attacker (**A**) grabs victim (**V**) from front under arms.

V immediately delivers double palm strike to **A**'s ears, causing him to release grip.

V then knees strikes **A**'s groin.

V grabs **A**'s head and slams it into her knee.

Defense Against Bear Hug
(from rear—over arms)

Attacker (**A**) grabs victim (**V**) in rear bear hug over his arms.

V side steps to his strong side and delivers chop strike to **A**'s groin with his weak hand.

V applies elbow strike to **A**'s solar plexus.

V strikes **A** in face with fist.

V shifts weight and steps behind **A**, grabbing behind **A**'s knees pulling **A** up and over his rear leg.

V drops **A** to the ground.

Defense Against a Bear Hug
From the Rear (under arms)

Attacker (**A**) grabs Victim (**V**) from behind in bear hug under **V**'s arms.

V forcefully hits **A** on wrist with his knuckle (see close up) and causes **A** to release grip.

OPTION: V may also stomp on **A**'s foot to gain release.

V then strikes **A** with elbow strike and maintains grasp on **A**'s hand.

V then steps out and to **A**'s side in counterclockwise motion and applies passive wrist-lock control technique.

V is now in position to follow up with stunning kick to **A**'s body if necessary.

Defense Against Front Choke #1

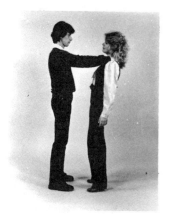

Attacker (**A**) applies front choke to victim (**V**).

V immediately strikes **A**'s elbows (45° angle) driving them into locked position...

and straightens out **A**'s arm, preventing choke.

OPTION: V grabs **A**'s wrist (directly behind wrists) pushing in.

V then shoves **A** straight back.

V applies knee strike to **A**'s midsection.

Defense Against Front Choke #2

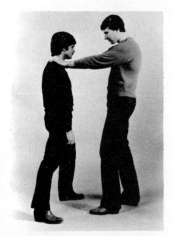

Attacker (**A**) applies front choke to victim (**V**).

V lowers his weight by bending knees causing **A** to lean forward, while clasping his hands.

V springs upward striking **A**'s arms inside, breaking **A**'s choke hold

V quickly strikes **A** in face.

V grabs **A**'s hair and pulls **A**'s head down while delivering knee strike to **A**'s face.

Defense Against Rear Choke

Attacker (**A**) grabs victim (**V**) from behind in choke hold.

V needs to breathe so he forces his hands between **A**'s arm and his throat.

V raises foot, ready to deliver stomp kick to **A**'s foot...

breaking **A**'s hold.

V then executes elbow strike to **A**'s solar plexus.

V pivots on left foot turning into **A**, using finger jab to eyes.

Children's Defense Against a Grab

Attacker (**A**) grabs Victim (**V**) by his arm in an attempt to abduct him. **V** immediately screams for help yelling that he's being kidnapped.

V bites **A**'s hand or wrist.

If **A** maintains grip then **V** should kick **A**'s closest shin, still screaming for help. **V** should run for safety upon release.

Children's Defense Against Abduction

Abductor (**A**) picks up victim (**V**) in abduction attempt.

(**V**) strikes **A** on nose and screams for help.

Defense Against Prone Attack

Attacker (**A**) knocks victim (**V**) to ground and sits on top of her pinning her arms down.

V concentrates her power and slides feet back under knees.

At same time, back bridges upper body and thrusts knees up.

Then toss **A** up and over, striking **A**'s groin with punch.

OPTIONS: If **A** pins **V**'s arms under him while possibly choking her, **V** is able to perform steps (2) and (3) while utilizing her arms to help toss **A** off, striking **A** in the groin in the process.

Passive Restraining Technique #1
Wrist Lock (opposite arm)

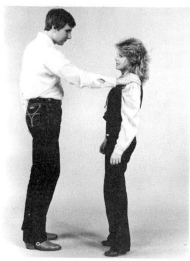

Attacker (**A**) grabs victim's (**V**) shoulder (opposite arm).

V strikes **A**'s upper arm muscle with one arm to weaken him or get him to release grab.

V peels **A**'s hand off with her other hand and completes wrist lock with both hands twisting **A**'s hand and wrist to gain control.

Passive Restraining Technique #2
Wrist Lock (cross arm)

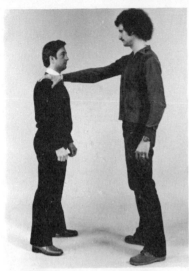

Attacker (**A**) grabs victim's (**V**) shoulder (cross arm).

V strikes (**A**) with one-handed punch to ribs and grips **A**'s hand with other hand.

V peels **A**'s hand off his shoulder while applying wrist lock.

V maintains wrist lock and runs behind while raising **A**'s hand high, and applying enough pressure to control **A**.

Passive Restraining Technique #3
Come Along

Restrainer (**R**) walks up behind troublemaker (**T**) with strong hand ready to grasp **T**'s hand.

R raises **T**'s hand shoulder-level.

Then he reaches across and presses down on **T**'s elbow pulling it into his chest.

R applies wrist lock to **T** while maintaining direct backward pressure on **T's** arm into **R**'s chest. **R**'s inside elbow can be lifted to convince **T** to move on command.

Passive Restraint Technique #4
Wrist Lock to ¼ Nelson

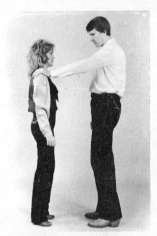

Attacker (A) grabs victim's (V) shoulder.

V strikes A's ribs with punch.

V reaches over with opposite hand and grabs A's hand.

V peels A's hand off with both hands.

V bends A's arm behind his back and grasps wrist with belt (see detail) sliding ¼ nelson under A's other arm for leverage.

Detail.

Defense Against Two Man Attack #1

Attacker one (**A1**) grabs victim (**V**) from behind while attacker two (**A2**) approaches. **V** grabs **A1**'s hand, trying to breathe.

V completes groin kick to **A2**.

V executes elbow strike to **A1** and begins to twist out of his grab.

V maintains control of **A1**'s hand.

V slides out and behind **A1**
and applies armlock.

V balances on **A1** then side
kicks **A2**'s knee.

Following up with knee strike
to **A1**'s chest.

Defense Against Two Man Attack #2

Attacker one (**A1**) grabs victim's (**V**) arm while attacker two (**A2**) approaches.

A2 reaches for **V** who strikes with groin kick.

V uses free arm to push **A2** down into awaiting knee strike.

V quickly strikes **A1** with finger jab to his eyes.

Defense Against Grab Using Keys

Attacker (**A**) grabs victim's (**V**) arm.

V spins into **A**, thrusting keys into his eyes.

Defense Against a Punch #1
Utilizing an Umbrella (or cane)

Attacker (**A**) attempts to punch victim (**V**).

V immediately side steps outside **A**'s line of attack, and raises umbrella to deflect **A**'s punch.

V hooks **A**'s arm, pulling it down and to the rear.

V then steps into **A** and strikes him in ribs with umbrella handle.

Defense Against a Punch #2
Utilizing an Umbrella

Attacker (**A**) attempts to punch victim (**V**).

V side steps outside **A**'s line of attack and raises umbrella to deflect **A**'s punch.

V strikes **A** on side of his knee, collapsing it.

V hooks **A**'s knee, pulling it up while pushing **A**...

over and down.

Defense Against Knife Attack #1
Utilizing an Umbrella (or cane)

Victim (**V**) walking to work is approached by attacker (**A**) with knife.

A raises knife to strike **V**. **V** drops his briefcase and assumes balanced stance.

A thrusts knife towards **V**, while **V** side steps attack and raises umbrella to strike **A**'s arm and deflect angle of thrust.

V hooks **A**'s arm, slides umbrella handle up to **A**'s wrist, and gains control over **A**'s arm.

V, using **A**'s forward momentum, swings **A**'s arm down into **A**.

V delivers baseball swing strike to **A** to incapacitate him.

Defense Against a Knife Attack #2

As Victim (**V**) walks to work, Attacker (**A**) approaches and threatens with knife.

V swings briefcase at **A**'s knife-hand in effort to deflect knife and escape.

Briefcase strikes **A**'s hand and knife drops to ground.

To be sure **A** does not continue attack, **V** follows up with groin kick.

Defense Against Knife Attack #3

As Victim (**V**) walks to work, Attacker (**A**) approaches and threatens with knife.

V raises briefcase to deflect knife attack.

V jams **A**'s knife hand against his body.

V then follows up with a head strike with briefcase.

Defense Against Knife Attack #4

As Victim (V) walks to work, Attacker (A) approaches and threatens with knife.

V immediately raises hands to block attack and side-steps to prevent stabbing.

V allows A's momentum to continue, assisting in downward motion. . .

driving knife into A.

V raises inside hand and prepares to strike A.

Defense Against Knife Attack #5

Attacker (**A**) prepares to stab Victim (**V**) with knife.

A slashes past **V** who jumps back and away from **A**.

V quickly slides into **A**, deflecting then grabbing **A**'s arm.

(open view)

V turns into **A**, and wedges himself between **A**'s body and arm, maintaining control, and breaks **A**'s arm by pulling it across his body. **A** drops knife.

V delivers elbow strike to **A**.

NOTE: The higher **V** raises **A**'s arm, the more pressure applied.

Defense Against Attack in and Auto

Victim (**V**) enters vehicle unaware of Attacker (**A**).
V has keys in hand.

A grabs **V** from behind.

V raises car keys.

V drives keys into **A**'s face, and **A** releases **V**. **V** jumps out and runs for help.

Conclusion

Nobody can force you to get involved in crime prevention. That's your decision. But isn't it much easier to get involved now, before a crime is experienced, than later after a son or daughter, husband or wife has become just another cold statistic?

Get involved, become aware, establish prevention, develop confidence and tell crime to go take a hike!

It's time to get tough with crime by denying it the opportunity to exist and function within our society. Our motto should be, "Prevention today for a safer tomorrow."

Crime Terms Defined

Aggravated Assault—Unlawful threat or attempt to inflict bodily injury or death by means of a deadly or dangerous weapon with or without actual infliction of any injury.

Arrest—The act of depriving an individual of his or her liberty by legal authority. The seizing of a person into the custody of the law for the purpose of charging that person with a criminal offense.

Assault—Unlawful intentional inflicting, or attempted or threatened inflicting, of injury upon the person of another.

Burglary—Unlawful entry of any fixed structure, vehicle, or vessel used for regular residence, industry, or business, with or without force, with intent to commit a felony or larceny.

Citizen's Arrest—The taking of a person into physical custody by a witness to a crime other than a law enforcement officer for the purpose of delivering him or her to the physical custody of a law enforcement officer or agency.

Consumer Fraud—Deception of the public with respect to the cost, quality, purity, safety, durability, performance, effectiveness, dependability, availability, and adequacy of choice relating to goods or services offered or furnished, and with respect to credit or other matters relating to terms of sales.

Criminal Homicide—Causing the death of another person without legal justification or excuse.

Deadly Weapon—An instrument designed to inflict serious bodily injury or death, or capable of being used for such a purpose.

Disturbing the Peace—Unlawful interruption of the peace, quiet, or order of a community, including offenses called "disorderly conduct," "vagrancy," "loitering," "unlawful assembly," and "riot."

Embezzlement—The misappropriation, misapplication, or illegal disposal of legally entrusted property by the person(s) to whom it was entrusted, with intent to defraud the legal owner or intended beneficiary.

Extortion—Unlawfully obtaining or attempting to obtain something of value from another by compelling the other person to deliver it by the threat of eventual physical injury or other harm to that person or his property or to a third person.

Felony—A criminal offense punishable by death, or by incarceration in a prison facility.

Forcible Rape—Sexual intercourse or attempted sexual intercourse with a female against her will, by force or threat of force.

Forgery—The creation or alteration of a written or printed document, which if validly executed would constitute a record of a legally binding transaction, with the intent to defraud by affirming it to be the act of an unknowing second person; also the creation of an art object with intent to misrepresent the identity of the creator.

Fraud—Offenses sharing the elements of practice of deceit or intentional misrepresentation of fact, with the intent of unlawfully depriving a person of his property or legal rights.

Involuntary Manslaughter—Causing the death of another person without intent to cause death, with recklessness or gross negligence, including by reckless or grossly negligent operation of a motor vehicle.

Kidnapping—Transportation or confinement of a person without authority of law and without his or her consent, or without the consent of his or her guardian, if a minor.

Larceny—Unlawful taking or attempted taking of property other than a motor vehicle from the possession of another, by stealth, without force and without deceit, with intent to permanently deprive the owner of the property.

Larceny-Theft—Unlawful taking, carrying, leading, or riding away by stealth of property, other than a motor vehicle, from the possession or constructive possession of another, including attempts.

Levels of Proof—The degrees of certainty required at different stages in the criminal justice process; their common names and characterizations are described below. To investigate requires "suspicion." To question or superficially search a suspect requires something more than suspicion but less than probable cause. To arrest and prosecute requires "probable cause." To convict requires "proof beyond a reasonable doubt."

Mayhem—Intentional inflicting of injury on another that causes the removal of, or seriously disfigures, or renders useless or seriously impairs the function of, any member or organ of the body.

Misdemeanor—An offense punishable by incarceration, usually in a local confinement facility, for a period of which the upper limit is prescribed by statute in a given jurisdiction, typically limited to a year or less.

Modus Operandi—A characteristic pattern of behavior repeated in a series of offenses that coincides with the pattern evidenced by a particular single person, or by a particular group of persons working together.

Motor Vehicle Theft—Unlawful taking, or attempted taking, of a self-propelled road vehicle owned by another, with the intent to deprive him of it permanently or temporarily.

Murder—Intentionally causing the death of another person without extreme provocation or legal justification or while committing or attempting to commit another crime.

Peeping Tom—A popular name for a person who trespasses for the purpose of observing persons inside a dwelling.

Personal Larceny with Contact—The theft or attempted theft by stealth of money or property from the immediate possession of a person without the use or threat of force.

Personal Larceny Without Contact—The theft or attempted theft by stealth of money or property of a person without direct contact between the victim and the offender.

Personal Robbery—The theft or attempted theft of money or property from the immediate possession of a person, by force or threat of force, with or without a weapon.

Probable Cause—A set of facts and circumstances that would induce a reasonably intelligent and prudent person to believe that a crime had been committed and that a particular person had committed it; reasonable grounds to make or believe an accusation. The evidence sufficient to establish probable cause at the time of arrest, and thus to justify the lawfulness of the arrest, can be less than that required to support prosecution. Thus an arrest can be lawful even though charges are later dismissed at a preliminary hearing for lack of probable cause.

Proof Beyond a Reasonable Doubt—Proof that does not amount to absolute certainty but leaves no reasonable doubt that the defendant committed the alleged crime(s), that is, a standard of proof in which evidence offered in court to prove an alleged set of facts must preclude every reasonable hypothesis except that one which it supports, that of the defendant's guilt.

Rape—Unlawful sexual assault or attempted assault of another person of the same or opposite sex, by force or the threat of force.

Robbery—The unlawful taking or attempted taking of property that is in the immediate possession of another by force or the threat of force.

Runaway—A juvenile who has been adjudicated by a judicial officer of a juvenile court as having committed the status offense of leaving the custody and home of his or her parents, guardians, or custodians without permission and failing to return within a reasonable length of time.

Self-Defense—The protection of oneself or one's property from unlawful injury or the immediate risk of unlawful injury; the justification for an act that would otherwise constitute an offense, which the person who committed it reasonably believed was necessary to protect self or property from immediate danger.

Sex Offense—All unlawful sexual intercourse, unlawful sexual contact, and other unlawful behavior intended to result in sexual gratification or profit from sexual activity.

Simple Assault—Unlawful intentional inflicting of less than serious bodily injury without a deadly or dangerous weapon.

Theft—Generally, any taking of the property of another with intent to permanently deprive the rightful owner of possession; in the broadest legal usage the name of the group of offenses having this feature: larceny, fraud, embezzlement, false pretenses, robbery, and extortion.

Threat—The declaration by words or actions of an unlawful intent to do some injury to another, together with an apparent ability to do so.

Truant—A juvenile who has been adjudicated by a judicial officer of a juvenile court as having committed the status offense of violating a compulsory school attendance law.

Vandalism—The destroying or damaging of, or attempting to destroy or damage the property of another without his consent, or public property, except by burning.

Venue—The geographical area in which a crime is committed, within which a court has jurisdiction; the geographical area (municipality, county, etc.) from which a jury is drawn and in which trial is held in a court action.

Victim—A person who has suffered death, physical or mental anguish, or loss of property as the result of an actual or attempted criminal offense committed by another person.

Voluntary Manslaughter—Intentionally causing the death of another with provocation that a reasonable person would find extreme without legal justification.

Bibliography

Flanagan, Timothy J.; van Alstyne, David J.; Gottfredson Michael R., eds. U.S. Department of Justice, Bureau of Justice Statistics. *"Sourcebook of Criminal Justice Statistics—1981."* Washington, D.C.: U.S. Government Printing Office, 1982.

Gardner, Thomas J. and Manion, Victor. *"Criminal Law; Principles, Cases, and Readings."* St. Paul, Minn: West Publishing Co., 1975.

Garofolo, James. U.S. Department of Justice, Law Enforcement Assistance Administration. *"Compensating Victims of Violent Crimes; Potential Costs and Coverage of a National Program."* Washington, D.C.: U.S. Government Printing Office, 1977.

Hochstedler, Ellen. U.S. Department of Justice, Bureau of Justice Statistics. *"Crime Against the Elderly in 26 Cities."* Washington, D.C.: U.S. Government Printing Office, 1981.

Lyford, George J. *"Boat Theft; A High-Profit/Low-Risk Business."* FBI Law Enforcement Bulletin, May, 1982, pp. 1-5.

Rand, Michael R. U.S. Department of Justice, Bureau of Justice Statistics. *"Violent Crime by Strangers."* Washington, D.C.: U.S. Government Printing Office, 1982.

U.S. Department of Justice, Bureau of Justice Statistics. *"Crime and the Elderly."* Washington, D.C.: U.S. Government Printing Office, 1981.

U.S. Department of Justice, Bureau of Justice Statistics. *"Dictionary of Criminal Justice Data Terminology."* 2d ed. Washington, D.C.: U.S. Government Printing Office, 1981.

U.S. Department of Justice, Federal Bureau of Investigation. *"Uniform Crime Reports"*—1976, 77, 78, 79, 80, 81, and 82. Washington, D.C.: U.S. Government Printing Office, 1982.

Index

Richard A. Fike is presently a federal agent for the U.S. Government. He has been involved in the field of law enforcement for the last ten years, in the U.S. Army, where he served as a Special Agent with Military Intelligence, and as a corporate investigator. In his spare time, he teaches self defense at local colleges and private agencies and law enforcement subjects at police/security academies. He is an expert in the martial arts and is Vice President of the Ohio Association for Forensic and Investigative Hypnosis.